Shades of Gray, Splashes of Color

A Thru-hike of
The Colorado Trail

Sherry,
May your "Happy
Trails" include the Colorado
Trail, before or after you
finish the AT! Enjoy

Bill Cooke

Bill Cooke

Shades of Gray, Splashes of Color: A Thru-hike of
The Colorado Trail

Printed in the USA

The map on page xii is reprinted with permission from the Colorado Trail Foundation

All photos are by the author

The author's original trail journal may be found on-line at www.trailjournals.com/CookerhikerCT11

Contact the author at Bill@cookerhiker.com

ISBN-13: 978-1494785710
ISBN-10: 1494785714

Dedication

To the women and men of The Colorado Trail Foundation—past, present, and future—who had and have the vision to conceive the Colorado Trail, the will to plan the trail's route, the patience in dealing with multiple government agencies and private parties, the sweat equity in constructing the trail, the devotion to ongoing trail maintenance and improvement, and the foresight to continually assess the trail's future. It is because of and through their efforts that the Colorado Trail exists today.

CONTENTS

CONTENTS

Author's Note

"Everything is blooming most recklessly; if it were voices instead of colors, there would be an unbelievable shrieking into the heart of the night."

Rainer Maria Rilke

"Smile O voluptuous coolbreathed earth!...Earth of the limpid gray of clouds brighter and clearer for my sake!"

Walt Whitman

T HIS BOOK RELATES my experience of hiking the 482-mile Colorado Trail in the summer of 2011. As such, it incorporates the physical aspects as well as the thoughts and feelings that ran through my mind as I hiked this trail. The meat of the book ("The Hike" section) is organized chronologically, but I have striven to avoid an overly rigid and tedious structure of Day 1, Day 2, Day 3, etc. Some of the transitions from one day to the next are readily apparent with clearly marked breaks while others simply blend from late afternoon or evening to the subsequent morning. For those hiker nerds who want to "cut to the chase" and simply *must* know each day's progress (where I started, where I ended, how many miles), this information is presented in Appendix 1.

In some instances, I offer observations and reflections beyond the narrow confines of the day-by-day hike, but this is not a work of deep philosophy. This narrative does flesh out some of my musings which occurred along the trail. But I haven't added any "new" thoughts, musings, etc. that didn't, to some extent, cross my mind during the hike itself. And it shouldn't need be said, but I'll say it: the adjectives and imagery that I invoke represent how I actually felt, not because they sound pleasing and/or "literary."

This book does not purport to be a formal guidebook to backpacking—the Colorado Trail or any other. Anyone interested in backpacking will find, scattered throughout the book, some hints and tips of what such an endeavor entails. But it does not contain a thorough, comprehensive discussion of gear or equipment or other important considerations when undergoing a hike of this magnitude. For those planning a Colorado Trail thru-hike in particular, the book will hopefully provide an idea of the environment, trail conditions, and options for re-supplying but again, other references should also be used. I have included some recommended references in Appendix 4.

Also, I have not delved into any detail about natural history such as the plants, flowers, and trees, nor the geological features, other than emphasizing how much I enjoyed every aspect of the Rocky Mountain eco-region. As I have stated in the book's "Pre-hike" section, I am not a scientist of any sort, nor pretend to be one. In a similar vein, the corridor through which the Colorado Trail passes possesses a rich human history which, while fascinating, is not addressed in this book.

Finally, referring to the quotations at the beginning of this Note, I wish to say a few words about why I chose the title and the related cover design.

Think Colorado—think mountains, specifically the Rocky Mountains. Images of them are etched on the state license plates. Flying into Denver, you see them looming in the west. Until ceasing operations in 2009, one of Denver's major newspapers was the *Rocky Mountain News*. John Denver sings *Rocky Mountain High*. The baseball team's name is the Colorado Rockies and their purple colors evoke the purple mountains majesty which are visible beyond their stadium's center field. Think the Colorado Trail—what else but the Rocky Mountains?

So one might expect that a book about thru-hiking the Colorado Trail would incorporate "mountains" in its title or subtitle. Shouldn't the cover photo include a range, perhaps headed by one or more peak over 14,000', affectionately known in Colorado outdoor life circles as "14ers?" Isn't that why one hikes the Colorado Trail—to get into the mountains? Didn't John Muir urge us to "Climb the mountains and get their good tidings?" Isn't that what it's all about?

Yes, it certainly is. I wouldn't have attempted to hike the Colorado Trail—much less write a book about it—if the trail proceeded down the state's eastern plains straight from Nebraska to Oklahoma. The Rocky Mountains are what it's all about.

And what is it about the Rockies that's so picturesque, so stunning, so inspiring? Would a series of thirteen and fourteen thousand-foot peaks have the same appeal if they were covered in a monochrome brown dirt or barren rock from top to bottom?

From the very first day when my hiking partner and I traversed through wildflowers of various hues and gazed at the afternoon sky's gray swirling clouds which changed every two minutes, displaying more patterns than imaginable, I was captivated by the colors and the shades of gray. As the hike progressed, the theme progressed. Every day, we encountered most colors of the spectrum—in meadows, in forests, on slopes, in dry almost desert-like country, and of course in alpine areas. Every day, shades of gray were manifested in the afternoon skies, in the different colored rocks and mountain slopes, in the tree trunks, even in the soil at times. It is these phenomena that make the summertime Colorado Rocky Mountains so exquisite and the experience of hiking the Colorado Trail so rewarding.

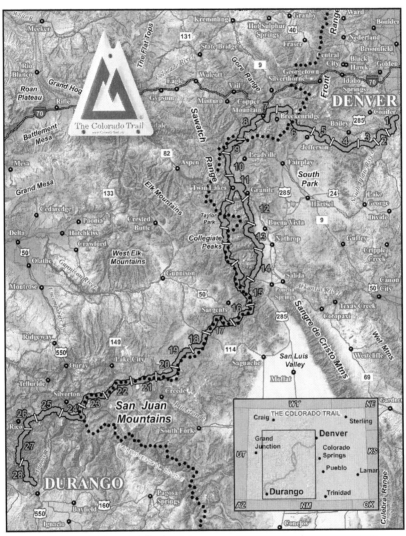

The Colorado Trail

"Keep close to Nature's heart ...and break clear away, once in a while, and climb a mountain or spend a week in the woods. Wash your spirit clean. None of Nature's landscapes are ugly so long as they are wild."

"How glorious a greeting the sun gives the mountains!"

"God never made an ugly landscape. All that the sun shines on is beautiful as long as it's wild..."

John Muir

Shades of Gray, Splashes of Color

Pre-Hike

First Thoughts

I
T'S EARLY SPRING OF 2011 and I've decided to thru-hike the Colorado Trail. So what does this entail?

I've been backpacking for over 30 years. I've hiked the entire Appalachian Trail (over 2,100 miles), making me reasonably competent to handle matters in the backcountry wilderness. All of the necessary gear is at hand—pack, tent, sleeping bag, clothes, stove for cooking, etc. I love the high mountains and have spent many a time camping and hiking short distances in alpine splendor. The internet age has produced easy access to an abundance of materials in the form of books, maps, and contacts through websites and chatrooms, all of which render planning much easier than a generation ago.

But can I hike this trail, that is "thru-hike" (hiking the entire trail "through" in one continuous trek) its 482 miles? In pragmatic terms, the odds are somewhat against me:

■ I'm 63 years old, less than ten years younger than my father's age when he passed away. Aerobically speaking, my physical condition is adequate but I still carry 20 pounds too much and in the wrong place. I have strong legs (my only physical asset) but virtually no upper body strength. My eyesight is poor. I've been treated for a herniated disk. Heart disease runs in my family, although my own blood pressure is consistently excellent.

■ Yes, I've hiked the entire Appalachian Trail (AT), but not as a thru-hike. Rather, I spent 29 years chasing that dream with my

3

longest single hike being 300 miles from Northern New Hampshire to the northern endpoint on Mt. Katahdin, Maine. At 482 miles, a Colorado Trail thru-hike thus amounts to a 50% increase over my previous high.

- I have backpacked at high elevations (greater than 10,000') three times and always experienced acclimation problems. Two of these were hikes of 3-4 nights in duration where elevation sickness forced a curtailment of schedule. The other and inevitably most comparable expedition was a 2006 attempt to hike the John Muir Trail (JMT) in California's High Sierra. The 150 miles that I hiked on this venerated trail covered only about two-thirds the distance. Again, the high elevation did me in; after I had seemingly succeeded on the first day ascending 6,000' of elevation to the first camp, the second day found me weak and gasping. Time taken for a necessary rest and further acclimation prevented me from completing the trail in my allotted time.

- Lots of little things can torpedo a long-distance hike, ranging from injuries and accidents to less-physical phenomena: fatigue, weariness with bad weather (and the Rockies receive a lot of rain), even boredom. To an easterner accustomed to wretched summer humidity, the Mountain West's excessive dryness is noticeably welcome, but it brings some downsides of its own such as scarce water, dry lips and skin leading to chafing, and more dust to keep out of one's lungs. Even my nostrils dried up early on my JMT hike, creating a frustrating itchiness.

But none of this changes my mind or my intentions. Nothing I have mentioned above is a showstopper. Actually, finishing the AT was probably a bigger leap for me. At retirement in 2003 from my accounting and financial management position at the U.S. Environmental Protection Agency, the 700 or so miles hiked on the AT to that point were limited to day-hikes and short backpacking trips never exceeding 4-5 days. I wanted to finish the AT "some day" but I couldn't fathom the concept of long-distance hiking—of having to worry about re-supply and transportation and durability to hike 100 miles, let alone 200 or 500 or 1,000 or 2,000 miles. AT thru-hikers, indeed any long-distance hikers, were an esteemed breed to me. I just assumed that the AT would take another 10 years or more to complete via my normal means of short hikes.

A paradigm shift occurred beginning in 2004 as I hiked distances of 100, then 185, then other long hikes culminating in my final 300 miles where I stood atop Katahdin in September 2005, astounded at my own accomplishment. Moreover, that stretch through Maine, especially the first 100 miles or so after crossing the border from New Hampshire, was the most difficult hiking I had ever undertaken, a fact not irrelevant to my plan to hike the Colorado Trail. One hypothesis was that aside from the very real concern of high elevation acclimation, nothing the Colorado Trail could throw my way would prove as difficult, as arduous, as the AT in Southwestern Maine.

I also considered the many rewards derived from a Rocky Mountain backpack. Thoughts of bright morning sunshine, colorful alpine flowers, lingering snowfields, high-elevation lakes and streams, scurrying marmots and pikas (and perhaps elk and if I'm lucky, bighorn sheep), groves of fascinating aspen trees, stately conifers like the Douglas firs, cool dry evenings (sandwiched around the inevitable afternoon thunderstorms and the fascinating shades of gray skies they engender), clean air, stupendous views as rewards for ascents up mountains and beyond treeline, early morning and late afternoon alpenglow—all are a clarion call to the hiker, the wanderer, the nature lover or anyone who appreciates the beauty of the outdoors.

On a practical level, backpacking among mountains—even the lower-elevation peaks of the eastern ranges—is a guaranteed way to lose weight and build aerobic conditioning. If you're not in shape beforehand, you will be after the first 100 miles. It's certainly more fun and rewarding than a treadmill or walking suburban streets! Unlike the home environment, you don't have the choice to opt out of the day's exercise ("I don't feel like doing the elliptical workout today"). On the trail, you wake up, hike up that mountain, and partake of the aforementioned rewards. And another practical note: what better (and less expensive) way to spend most of the summer than hiking the Rocky Mountains while the East, including my new home state of Kentucky, bakes in heat and humidity? When night falls, I want to sleep in fresh cool mountain air, not encased in the necessary evil of air conditioning.

I've been around long enough to realize this trek will feature highs and lows, literally and figuratively. That some things won't go as planned is a given, but how's that different from life? To paraphrase a theme attributed to more than one source: the biggest failure is when we don't try in the first place.

And it doesn't hurt that I have a hiking partner with whom I've hiked many times totaling hundreds of miles.

I've hiked the AT. I can hike the Colorado Trail.

So What is the Colorado Trail?

I T'S SURPRISING TO ME that when I mention hiking the Colorado Trail, many people respond with "Where is that?" "Uh, it's in Colorado." Okay, perhaps the linkage of "Colorado" with "Trail" is less than straightforward. Everyone has heard of the Appalachian Trail and likely the Pacific Crest Trail (PCT) as well. And everyone's heard of the river and probably aware that most of the length and watershed of the Colorado River lies outside the state of Colorado. It's not far-fetched, particularly for those not attuned to the strange outdoor recreation known as backpacking, to think that perhaps the Colorado Trail parallels the river.

Anyway, the short answer is that the Colorado Trail runs 486 miles mostly through the Rocky Mountains between the southwestern suburbs of Denver and a trailhead in the San Juan National Forest a few miles north of Durango. And where is Durango? Less than 25 miles north of the New Mexico border and about 70 miles as-the-crow-flies east of the Utah border, Durango boasts 17,000 residents and provides a gateway to Mesa Verde National Park, 35 miles to the west. So the Colorado Trail proceeds mostly on a southwest/northeast slant. Of course the trail meanders, twists, and turns like all mountain trails so that if you're constantly consulting your Global Positioning System, you'll find yourself going north sometimes when you're really hiking south.

Then there are those who have vaguely heard of the Colorado Trail with some familiarity. From such, the most frequent and (to me) unsurprising question is: "Is that the same as the Continental Divide Trail?" The short answer here is "In part." The Continental Divide Trail (CDT) is a legally-designated National Scenic Trail following the Continental Divide (imagine that!) between the Mexican and Canadian borders. "Legally-designated" means the CDT falls under the aegis of the federal government in furtherance of the National Trails System Act of 1968. This is not the case for the Colorado Trail which was built and is maintained by volunteers working for a private organization: The Colorado Trail Foundation. Of course, since nearly all of the Colorado Trail lies on federal lands, chiefly national forests, the foundation effectively works in partnership with the U. S. Forest Service.

And the trails do overlap, not surprising given that a large chunk of the CDT goes through Colorado. Specifically, 235 miles of the Colorado Trail's 486 miles run concurrent with the CDT in two disparate portions: a 100 mile stretch from Georgia Pass to Twin Lakes in the northern half, and a 135 mile section from the Monarch Crest (a day's hike south of the U.S. Route 50 crossing outside Salida) to the top of Elk Creek Canyon shortly before Silverton. The latter stretch is highly diverse, ranging from dry, almost plains-like terrain to the Colorado Trail's highest point amid alpine meadows well above treeline. Barely a year after my hike, the Colorado Trail was augmented by adding the CDT stretch between Twin Lakes and the Monarch Crest, resulting in 80 additional miles of trail. This "extension" in effect presents an alternative route but does not change the Colorado Trail's beginning and end points.

More basics about the Colorado Trail: its 486 miles pass through eight National

Near Leadville, Elk Ridge was our favorite section of the entire Colorado Trail

Forests and six officially-designated Wilderness Areas within those Forests. As I was to discover, not all (perhaps not even half) of the Colorado Trail traverses through high-elevation, above-treeline alpine meadows; there are significant stretches in dense forests of aspens and/or evergreens such as lodgepole pines and Douglas firs as well as open, dry chaparral. And contrary to a stereotype of western trails *vis-a-vis* eastern trails in which the former are said to be more often on dirt paths than the rockfields of the latter, the Colorado Trail includes some stretches of rocky footing, notably on open talus slopes and in portions of the forested areas.

The Colorado Trail passes through several major watersheds such as the Platte, Arkansas, and Rio Grande all east of the Continental Divide, and the Animas which flows into Lake Powell via the San Juan River west of the Divide. Throughout the trail's corridor, the hiker encounters a broad diversity of trees, grasses, smaller shrubs and plants, a few succulents, and most beauteously, wildflowers of every hue. Not being a botanist, ecologist, or any other type of -ist, it would be pretentious of me to elaborate more; the important point is how this variety of flora makes for such an enjoyable experience. Of the trail's geological features, I refer interested readers to a six-page section in the Colorado Trail Foundation's guidebook entitled "The Rocks Along the Colorado Trail."

Back to the Colorado Trail Foundation: based in Golden, CO (famous or infamous as the home of Coors Beer), the foundation is the successor to a previous organization who conceived and began planning the Colorado Trail in 1974. Working with only a small staff, the non-profit foundation manages the trail through a vast network of volunteers who "adopt" sections of the trail for maintenance and monitoring and serve on trail crews for major construction or restoration. Virtually all funding emanates from private sources: member dues, donations and the like with little-to-no governmental assistance. And while any maintenance of a hiking trail entails much "sweat equity," the Colorado Trail's Wilderness Areas present special challenges. Aside from the difficulty of accessing their remote locations, federal restrictions governing Wilderness activities prohibit the use of chain saws and other mechanized equipment. Of course, the foundation and its volunteers must coordinate extensively with the U.S. Forest Service and other public agencies as well as private landowners in some stretches.

That the trail exists and is mostly in fine condition with good signs, bridges over creeks, cleared treadway, etc. is a testimony to the foundation's ardor and effectiveness. Indeed, of the challenges I faced in writing this book, the easiest decision was the dedication. Drawing on the imagery employed by Thomas Jefferson and countless other philosophers, my admiration and respect for the Colorado Trail Foundation and all people associated with it springs from both the head and the heart.

Another Colorado Trail Foundation endeavor is *The Colorado Trail*, the aforementioned very helpful and detailed guidebook. This was to become my "Bible" both in planning and during the hike itself. The book divides the trail into 28 segments of varying length ranging from 11 miles to the 32-mile stretch from Kenosha Pass to State Route 9 outside Breckenridge. The segments are numbered 1-28 in a north-to-south direction (see Appendix 2 for a list of the segments). With one exception, each segment has road access of some sort at both ends, plus some segments feature road access in the middle as well. Now "road access" doesn't always mean that your buddy or in-laws can drive at 55 mph in their fully-equipped RV to greet you with a latte or beer or both to celebrate each segment's completion; many such access points are remote Forest Service roads only reachable using four-wheel-drive vehicles. The most frequently-occurring guidebook words describing these access points are "limited parking," "steep and rocky," "challenging"—you get the picture. However, perspective and context count for something; when compared to the JMT, the Colorado Trail is quite easy to reach and re-supply for most of its length.

The guidebook groups the 28 "segments" into five "sections" but drawing on my hike experience, I've immodestly designated seven "sections" which seemed logical, i.e. not completely contrarian, arbitrary, or an exercise in second-guessing the foundation. They are, from north-to-south (the direction of my hike) as follows:

1. **Foothills and Forests** — start of the trail to Kenosha Pass (U.S. Route 285) or Segments 1-5, characterized mostly by lower elevations and/or dense forests;

2. **Reaching 12 K** — Kenosha Pass to Tennessee Pass (U.S. Route 24) outside of Leadville; this is Segments 6-8, where much of the trail is above treeline;

3. **Rocks of the Rockies** — Tennessee Pass to Clear Creek, Segments 9-11, where the rocky footing in some parts reminded me of northern New England;

4. **Steep and Steeper** — Clear Creek to U.S. Route 50 (near Salida), Segments 12-14, which includes some of the most difficult, i.e. steepest elevation change (ups and downs) of the entire trail;

5. **Dry Heartland** — Route 50 to the Eddiesville Trailhead, Segments 15-19, where water availability is the preeminent challenge;

6. **Alpine Again** — Eddiesville Trailhead to Molas Pass outside Silverton (U.S. Route 550) along Segments 20-24, where the longest, most extensive above-treeline stretch includes the Colorado Trail's highest point at 13,271'; and finally,

7.   **A Southwestern Feel** — Molas Pass to the southern terminus near Durango, Segments 25-28, an area where the reddish rocks and some of the vegetation were reminiscent, to me at least, of parts of Arizona and New Mexico.

The guidebook points out a metric which for some hikers may fall into "TMI" or a daunting statistic that the faint-hearted might find discouraging: a southbound thru-hiker will ascend 89,354' over the 486 miles. Because the southern terminus near Durango lies at a greater elevation above sea level than the northern endpoint, the northbound thru-hiker ascends "only" 87,892' which of course represents the descent faced by the southbounder. So under the overly-simplistic assumption that you're hiking uphill half the time, the southbounder's ascent amounts to 368 vertical feet per mile. That may not seem too bad (for example, ascending Mt. Katahdin on the AT in Maine amounts to 4,200 vertical feet in just 5.2 miles) but not every mile on the Colorado Trail (or any mountain trail system, east or west) is "equal." A few gradual, near-level portions have an ameliorating effect on the steep portions (e.g. the Collegiate Peaks in Segments 12 and 13) such that the 368' simple average is virtually meaningless.

My hiking partner and I relied on other sources for both preliminary planning and for reference during the hike itself. The foundation also produces *The Colorado Trail Databook* (essentially a pocket-sized condensed summary of milepoints) and *The Colorado Trail Map Book*, an atlas of maps covering the entire corridor with more detail than those included in the guidebook. Another highly useful resource is an on-line guide authored by Paul "Mags" Magnanti, a transplanted New Englander living in Colorado and an experienced outdoorsman who has hiked not only the Colorado Trail but the so-called Triple Crown of long distance trails: AT, CDT, and the Pacific Crest Trail (PCT). Mags' guide is particularly useful in logistical planning, a challenge in any long-distance hike. Mags is active in the Colorado Trail community; in fact, he has authored a piece on lightweight backpacking in the guidebook. Yet another helpful source was the Colorado Trail forum on the AT-oriented chatroom WhiteBlaze.net. Specific links to all of these resources are in Appendix 4.

A major logistical concern for a hike of this magnitude is transportation for both the beginning and ending termini of the trail. For us, friends provided rides to the northern starting point and from the ending point in Durango. So our major logistical issue was re-supplying ourselves with food and other items for the course of the 482 miles. Nowhere does the Colorado Trail literally pass through a town. The most accessible such place is crossing CO Route 9 a few miles from Breckenridge where a local (and free) bus service whisks you into town. Otherwise for your resupply needs and the creature comforts of a town stop, you walk or you hitchhike anywhere from a mile (Twin Lakes, locale of a small General Store *cum* Post Office and not much more) to 13 miles on U.S. Route 50 into Salida just past the trail's halfway point (quick: what's the only U.S. Highway intersected by both the AT and Colorado Trail? Answer: U.S. 50).

And then there's Creede, a small town with nice facilities (motels, outfitter, grocery store, restaurants), but where you hike 1.5 miles down a side trail to a four-wheel drive road heavily rutted, hoping that someone will happen along in a jeep and take you the remaining 8.5 miles into town. Why would you put yourself through that hassle? Because Creede is the first realistic opportunity for R&R&R (resupply, rest, recreation) after Salida, a trail distance of 90 miles. The guidebook helpfully points out the conundrum hikers face as the book's most frequent phrase in describing the Salida-to-Creede segments is "no convenient resupply." You can continue hiking past San Luis Pass (the turnoff side trail to Creede) for another 15 miles to a paved highway at Spring Creek Pass. From there, your choice is to hitch 33 miles to Creede or 17 miles to Lake City, a smaller community, but Spring Creek Pass is described as a "tough hitch."

Pouring over the materials and preparing spreadsheets just like John Muir (not!), we decided on eight points for resupply where we would mail ourselves packages (known in hiker parlance as "maildrops"), in some cases supplementing the package contents with additional supplies purchased in "town" such that it was. Three of the eight were combination Post Office/General Stores in small communities, the aforementioned Twin Lakes being one such example. The other five were hostels or motels in, comparatively-speaking, mighty metropolises to which we sent our maildrops and stayed a night or two.

In addition to food, my particular need was canisters of a

The Simple Lodge & Hostel was a welcome respite in Salida

propane-butane fuel mix for my ultralight Coleman stove. Colorado being very much an outdoors-oriented state, there were outfitters in nearly all of our stops and even the Twin Lakes General Store carried canisters. Of course hikers crave "real" food after days on the trail and we usually weren't disappointed in the restaurant selections in most of the communities where we spent the night—Breckenridge, Leadville, Salida, and Silverton. These four locations also featured hostels where not only were the rates "hiker friendly," i.e. cheap, but also afforded the opportunity to mix and mingle with other afficionados of the outdoor life in the mountains, mainly cyclists. As a smaller community, Creede's restaurants were more limited but at least the town featured a decent motel as well as an outfitter selling the fuel canisters.

Before leaving here, I'll address the numerical discrepancy that some sharp-eyed readers, likely engineers or accountants like me (actually an ex-accountant), may be hung up on. Earlier I referred to "thru-hiking" 482 miles, but isn't the Colorado Trail 486 miles? No typo here, the trail is 486 miles. But during all of 2011, the trail's north entrance at Waterton Canyon outside Denver was closed because of a major maintenance project on the Strontia Springs Dam which lies several miles up the canyon. This closure effectively removed nearly eight miles of Trail for the year. The Colorado Trail Foundation's recommended alternative means to access the Colorado Trail was a side trail named the Indian Creek Trail, emanating from the Indian Creek Trailhead (imagine that!) about ten miles west of the town of Sedalia. Since this was an officially-designated alternate route complete with signs and the foundation's logo, I considered the four mile Indian Creek Trail part of my Colorado Trail hike. Thus 486 miles minus the eight mile closure plus the four mile Indian Creek Trail yields 482 miles. That's the number in my journal, so it's correct!

Indian Creek Trailhead

"WE'VE GONE ABOUT ten miles now. There's the sign. We should be there before too long."

We had passed the sign confirming our entry into Pike National Forest. The voice was mine. From the back seat. The car was winding its way along a county highway which had just become a Forest Service road.

"It should say 'Indian Creek Trailhead Parking' and there'll probably be horses around. I think there's a corral. There it is, up on the right. Got to be it."

It was Sunday, July 24, 2011.

In the front seat were the "two Keiths"—two friends of mine, both named Keith, whom I had known for a combined total of 80 years. They had never met each other until yesterday but both shared connections with me, not just general friendship and life experiences together, but also in the impact of backpacking on our lives.

Keith Davis was at the wheel. We met in the summer of 1975 as co-workers at the Defense Contract Audit Agency in Silver Spring, MD. I had just transferred to the branch office where he worked and before long, we had become friendly. As auditors of government contractors, we didn't work side-by-side on the same jobs but talked about them and about our lives and careers. I had recently passed the CPA examination to which he aspired, and he was studying for his Masters at George Washington University, where influenced by him, I later enrolled for my own MBA. It seemed like we were on the same wave length, in sync for many things.

16

Memorial Day weekend of 1977 was approaching and I brought the subject up:

"So, what are you doing for the weekend?"

"No plans yet. How about you?"

"I'd really like to go up to Vermont and backpack about 50 miles of the Appalachian Trail."

His response was what I secretly hoped for: "Vermont sounds good. Do you mind if I join you?"

And the trip was on. Despite hiking as much as I could, I had never done an overnight backpack trip but I had pitched tents and camped, cooked meals in a campsite, and possessed the necessary, if only basic, gear: backpack, boots, sleeping bag, portable stove, cooking utensils, and a two person tent considered modern and lightweight at the time. Keith on the other hand had done none of the above nor had he any gear to speak of. Looking back, I don't even remember how we outfitted him. But he was eager and enthusiastic as we planned the trip and drove up to Vermont in his car.

Our planned 52-mile hike ended up being about 39 miles. We took a wrong turn and hiked extra miles. We were besieged by mosquitos. We were grateful for no rain, but the temperatures were unseasonably hot. Sore feet came from stepping on too many rocks and roots while our knees suffered from the steep descents. I may have been more experienced, but I was in horrible shape aerobically speaking, and struggled with ordinary ascents that 30 years later I handled easily in my 60s. And Keith was a trooper, not complaining, keeping a positive spirit, and patiently awaiting me at the top of climbs as I struggled. Here was this new experience for him—coping with a lot of things that didn't go as planned, that inflicted pain, that wasn't exactly a paragon of holiday weekend relaxation. We were both exhausted and relieved that the hike was finished.

It was a smashing success.

Keith caught the bug; he was back in Vermont with another friend a few weeks later. 1978 found us in Vermont again, backpacking another stretch. And another stretch in Pennsylvania in the fall. And back to Vermont for the next three years until we had completed the Long Trail, the 272-mile Massachusetts-to-Canada pathway up the spine of Vermont's Green Mountains whose southernmost 100 miles coincide with the AT.

Over the years we hiked together over much of the AT in Virginia as well as the White Mountains in New Hampshire. And as our careers progressed, we each had opportunities to help the other professionally. In 1978, I applied for a job with the U. S. Environmental Protection Agency (EPA) where Keith had started working a few months earlier. He had apprised me of the opening and his recommendation helped me secure the position. I worked for the EPA in various capacities for the next 25 years until my 2003 retirement. After earning a law degree, Keith left the government in 1981 for a series of private sector jobs. After his 1986 wedding (in which I was his best man), I received an employment feeler from a company I respected. "No thank you, I'm not interested, but I can recommend someone who I think is just who you need."

Keith got that job, which in turn led to opportunities that ultimately resulted in his relocation to Colorado and the eventual establishment of his own highly successful law practice. So we didn't see each other much as the years went by, but in 2002 he flew to Burlington, VT where we rendezvoused and enjoyed a 25-year anniversary reprise of our first backpacking trip. And I thought about that first trip: if not for Keith's positive outlook at the time, more sanguine than mine, would I have continued backpacking? I'd like to think "yes" but I can't be sure.

And though our contact had been limited as the years went on, Keith didn't hesitate when I phoned him about our planned Colorado Trail hike and asked him three questions:

"I'm planning to drive out. Can I store my car at your house or office?"

18

"Could we crash the night before at your house—just one night? There's two of us."

"Could you drive us to the trailhead?" (Keith lives in Evergreen, a western suburb of Denver).

All three answers were "Sure, no problem."

So on this warm sunny Sunday, Keith was driving us to the trailhead where we would start our 482-mile sojourn through the Colorado Rockies. The "us," "we," and "our" refers to me and my hiking partner who now occupied the passenger front seat, the other Keith, a.k.a. "Northern Harrier."

Fellow natives of New Jersey, Keith Bance and I had met in early 1967 when we were a sophomore and freshman respectively at Susquehanna University in Pennsylvania, finding ourselves in the same fraternity "pledge" class. A former varsity cross-country runner, he was tall, slender, and athletic, traits which he still retains 45 years later. We became friends and the following year, room-mates of sort (he had to pass through my room to get to his) and talked academics and life. Ironically, neither of us brought up, or likely even thought about, hiking and camping in the woods, al-though I had been aware of the Appalachian Trail's existence since pre-teen years and had even walked on parts of it.

As is often the case with college friends, graduation meant sep-aration and in those days, military service was often involved. Both of us served in the military after college and then went on with our lives, Keith eventually settling in the Philadelphia suburbs and me in the Maryland suburbs of Washington, D.C. Coinciden-tally, we both lived in our respective state's Montgomery County. We saw each other once at a college reunion in the mid-1970s, but otherwise our contact was limited to annual Christmas cards with only brief notes of what was going on.

It was sometime in the late 1990s when through the card ex-changes, we became aware of our mutual interest in backpacking. By then, I had hiked several hundred miles of the AT while Keith had hiked much of New Hampshire's rugged White Mountains.

My retirement came first, occurring in May 2003 after which I stepped up my AT backpacking in hopes of "some day" finishing the 2,184 mile trail but still via the short 4-5 day stretches which had been my norm. Hiking several hundred miles where one had to deal with transportation and re-supplying was out of my element; doing an AT thru-hike was inconceivable, not to mention partially redundant since I had already hiked about 700 miles. But even as a "mere" section-hiker, I decided to partake of an AT tradition and take on a "trail name" before I got stuck with one not of my choosing. Thus was born "Cookerhiker," chosen because (1) likely no one else used this name; (2) it incorporated my name and my recreational passion in a way that both hiker and non-hiker friends would recognize; and, (3) I like to cook, although not usually of the gourmet variety while on the trail.

Keith had previously announced his intention to thru-hike the AT. As 2003 wound down, Keith retired, informed me he was starting on Leap Day of 2004, and asked if I wanted to accompany him. Reflexively, I answered "no" for several reasons, but I offered to drive him down to Springer Mountain, Georgia (locale of the AT's southern terminus) and hike to the summit with him. Afterwards, I planned to depart for warmer climes while he began his six month trek. He accepted, we were on, and on New Year's Day 2004, we met at my Silver Spring, MD, house for some planning. It was our first face-to-face meeting in 30 years.

As our departure time neared, I thought more and more about using this opportunity to hike portions of the AT I had never hiked, indeed never seen. Perhaps I could prove to myself that I could hike more than 50 miles at a clip. So taking the plunge, I asked Keith about joining him for maybe the first 100 miles to a road crossing in Western North Carolina. His ready response: "I think it would be **great** if you would join me."

On a beautiful sunny cool-not-cold day that was the quadrennial February 29th, we stood atop Springer Mountain. Ten days later having endured rain, fog, cold temperatures, high winds, snow, the constant up-and-down of the AT in Georgia, occasional crowds of would-be thru-hikers, and the chagrin at discovering ourselves in a dry county when we ordered a pizza at a town stop, we pulled into Rainbow Springs Campground near Franklin, North Carolina with 100 miles under our slackened belts. A rare feeling swept over me, reflecting a paradigm shift: I had overcome a hurdle and was now confident, ready to hike more miles, big miles. Which I did. 18 months and hundreds of miles later, I crossed a road in Northern New Hampshire commencing what proved to be my longest and most arduous backpacking trip ever—300 miles through rugged Northern New England forests and mountains to stand atop Maine's Mt. Katahdin with the AT and its 2,184 miles behind me.

Through serendipity, happenstance, whatever, Keith had played a pivotal role in my becoming a long-distance backpacker. Who's to say what would have transpired if I hadn't joined him that day in Georgia? I doubt I'd be undertaking the Colorado Trail now. But the munificence may have been bilateral. Keith had prepared extensively—physically, mentally, psychologically—for his 2004 thru-hike. He had followed the AT tradition by taking on a trail name. Keith is an avid birder and since he was from the north and hiking north, "Northern Harrier" suited him fine. He didn't foresee how many of his fellow hikers, who were unfamiliar with avian nomenclature, thought his name was "Hairier"—not surprising since nearly all male hikers become "hairier" as their faces don't meet a razor for months.

Notwithstanding his preparations, Keith or "Northern Harrier," as he'll now be dubbed, was very grateful for my presence in these first 10 days. A good start to any hike always helps set the tone, especially when planning to walk 2,184 miles. Discovering from the outset that our paces were similar and compatible, the companionship helped his morale as well as mine. Each of us felt a confidence boost as the days and miles passed by. When we reached that road crossing in Western North Carolina, Northern Harrier

21

joked that he would now be forced to consult the maps and guide, a role I had unconsciously assumed. Up to that point, we had been satisfied with our ten mile-per-day pace, but subsequently Northern Harrier turned things up a notch and ended atop Mt. Katahdin on August 29, 2004. And to round out our AT experiences, just as I hiked up Springer Mountain at the start of his hike, he accompanied me up Katahdin when I completed the AT in 2005.

It's axiomatic that friends and/or colleagues in everyday life, even those who've known each other for decades, don't necessarily make the best hiking partners. In his seminal book about thru-hiking the AT (published at the beginning of the 1970s' backpacking craze when very few books of this genre existed), Ed Garvey described his decision to hike alone, contrary to all the well-meaning advice at the time. He cited an account of two early AT thru-hikers:

"On the Trail, 'molehills' can become 'mountains', and on more than one occasion, we found ourselves acting stupidly childish, although we had worked together for two years."

Without question, my joining Northern Harrier for those ten days was risky along those lines, more so for him than me. Our loose friendship across the miles and timespan of 37 years counted for virtually nothing in predicting how we'd actually hike together. But it worked—on the AT, for the northern half of Vermont's Long Trail (170 miles), for the 70-mile Laurel Highlands Trail of Southwestern Pennsylvania (in winter), for 130 miles of other trails in Northern Pennsylvania, and now, we hoped, for the Colorado Trail's 482 miles. More than once, we heard the question: "Will you guys still be friends after this hike?"

We'd find out. The car pulled into a parking place in the lot amid plenty of other vehicles, many with bike racks, reminding us that today was a weekend day near the metropolis of arguably the most outdoors-oriented state in America. Ample signs complete

Mile Zero starts at the Indian Creek Trailhead.

with the Colorado Trail logo told us we were in the right place. For 2011 at least, the trail starts here.

For all my backpacking experience, I'm not reluctant to admit that apprehension always strikes at this stage: a long hike is about to begin, there's no turning back, we have a lot ahead of us. And at this particular moment, we both felt a physical anxiety. Northern Harrier often experiences stomach ailments, some of which had occurred each morning beginning with our 1,200 mile drive to Keith Davis's house from my Lexington, KY, home. This morning was the worst thus far, causing a delay in our starting time while he visited a clinic and emerged with a prescription.

As for me, it started last evening when Keith took us on a sightseeing drive to the side road entrance for Mt. Evans, one of Colorado's "14ers." By the time we descended from the 9,000' level to Idaho Springs where we enjoyed a "last supper" at Tommyknocker's Brew Pub, I found myself breathing more heavily, even at Keith's Evergreen house situated at 7,500'. Now on the morning of our hike, though well below 7,000', the breathing was still more laborious than it should have been.

But we were ready, secure in knowing that like an athlete preparing for a "big game," or an actor getting ready for opening night, or a speaker about to address a large audience, or an accountant about to deliver an important briefing to senior management (the latter two scenarios of which I had done), the nerves would dissipate shortly after the action began.

The Hike

Foothills and Forests — Indian Creek Trailhead to Kenosha Pass

"To an easterner, 10K seems so high, it must be alpine, right?
Wrong!"
Day 4 — July 27, 2011

AVING TAKEN THE OBLIGATORY start-of-the-hike photos, Keith drove off while Northern Harrier and I contemplated the sunny path before us, flanked by lush grasses and blooming wildflowers. It was 12:18 pm when we took our first steps.

The day had rapidly warmed. Not knowing our starting elevation, we shouldn't have been surprised when the Indian Creek Trail led steadily downhill. Some hikers claim to not know or care what lies ahead, terrain-wise. Just point them to the trail and they hike. Up, down, whatever—take what comes. It's just walking, right? I wish that my sentiments were likewise, but I like to look at a map. I want to see how much up/down I'm doing: XXX feet (or more likely, X,XXX feet) of elevation over Y miles. The Colorado Trail guidebook features "elevation profiles" for each segment. As an easier (lazier?) means than studying a contour map, these profiles show the trail as a left-to-right line zig-zagging up and down over a horizontal scale of miles and vertical scale of feet. The zig-zag allows you to clearly see the steep portions and thus plan accordingly. The "plan," of course, consists of nothing more than psyching yourself up or hand-wringing.

But there was no elevation profile for the 4.4-mile Indian Creek Trail. All we knew is that for two miles under a hot sun with only occasional shade from the pine trees, we hiked downhill amongst a variety of wildflowers. They included aster-like daisies whose yellow centers perfectly complemented the lavender petals, brilliant purple thistle, Queen Anne's lace, and others I couldn't identify. Ripe red raspberries provided an unexpected culinary delight.

Being a weekend, others shared the trail with us as we met numerous mountain bikers, a few day-hikers, and some horseback riders ascending up the gentle slope. In my reading and research beforehand, I knew we'd see mountain bikers and frankly, I didn't know what to expect. There are stories of tensions with hikers and diatribes by the latter of the bikers' alleged damage to the treadway. But on this first day, our encounters with bikers were positive as they were to be on the entire hike.

Meanwhile, the increasing presence of clouds cooled things off—not atypical for Colorado. The stereotype of clear and sunny mornings giving way to cloudy afternoon skies followed by thunderstorms appeared true-to-form on this first day.

Crossing Bear Creek (a tributary of the South Platte River) twice, we began our first ascent. Feeling queasy all morning, I slowed to a crawl with frequent rest stops despite the slope's fairly gentle nature. Elevation? Poor sleep? Conditioning? A combination of all three? Whatever the reason, my fatigue and laborious breathing was decelerating our progress. And this was only the first day, a short-mileage day at that! I wondered how I'd do tomorrow. Usually I didn't have a problem at 6-7,000' but maybe age was affecting my ability to acclimate? Sure, I had felt some effects yesterday after Keith had driven us to the 9,000' level, but we weren't even close to that elevation now.

After the ascent and a ridgewalk featuring raindrops and distant thunder along with cooler temperatures, the Indian Creek trail ended at its junction with the Colorado Trail at an area called Lenny's Rest. A left turn led us downhill again, a steep descent in which I fell and wrenched my already-injured upper right arm in the process. Another intersection with Bear Creek brought us to appealing-looking campsites which called our names. Thus ended Day 1's hike with a mere 5.2 miles in the books.

And that was fine with both of us. The viability of our hiking partnership rests on several elements of compatibility. Northern Harrier and I both like short-mileage days in the beginning of a long hike, i.e. we don't start out with 15 or even 10 miles out-of-the-box. Let our 60-something bodies adjust! We're also both early, first-light risers and neither of us like to hike late into the evening, although we will if circumstances necessitate such. We observe "hiker midnight" which usually means bedtime before dark, sometimes pretty soon after dinner. And most importantly, we generally maintain the same overall pace. Note the terms "generally" and "overall" —they're important later.

Our campsites were pretty decent: reasonably shady on a slight slant and adjacent to a good water source in Bear Creek. For my part, taking it easy in camp was necessary since I still was not breathing normally and felt occasional nausea and light-headedness. How could it not be elevation-related?

Northern Harrier's accouterments included two new major pieces of gear whose acquisition was necessitated by some miserable experiences on our hike last fall on the Susquehannock Trail in Northern Pennsylvania. What can be "miserable" about the Great Outdoors, especially in the October foliage of the eastern deciduous forest? How about a leaky tent and not-warm-enough sleeping bag? His new Tarptent looked pretty effective as well as light; it weighed considerably less than my Mountain Hardwear two-person tent. Along with his new sleeping bag, he probably packed 10 pounds less than me.

Bugs at the campsite were merely annoying, not chomping on us, not interested in our blood. Firing up my efficient canister stove for the first time, I ate my whole wheat macaroni and cheese dinner slowly and felt slightly better after supper while still fretting about tomorrow. What I really needed was a good night's sleep. With a 7:00 pm bedtime ("hiker midnight," although it wasn't even dark yet), we planned a 5:00 am rising. A very warm night tempted me to start shirtless atop my sleeping bag, a position I retained halfway through the night. The mugginess reminded me of the East!

* * * * *

RISING AT 5:15 AM, we were on the trail at 6:40. What a difference one day and a good night's sleep made! I felt much better right at the onset, displaying strength on the immediate uphill which began the day. We reaped the benefit of an early start with cool temperatures and clear skies. Ascending from the densely-wooded lower elevation, we reached a drier forest whose openness afforded good views. Far ahead we could see a massive-looking rock formation named Chair Rocks, not recognizing it at the time and not knowing it would be today's goal. I really reveled in this morning's ridge walking—it seemed more like the Colorado of western hiking whereas yesterday's dense forest, foliage, and humid atmosphere seemed eastern-like.

Hiking at a more rapid-than-expected pace, we came to open areas with views of the South Platte River, our intended destination. This was not the "mile wide, inch deep" muddy run of Eastern Colorado and Nebraska, but a sparkly and clean-looking mountain river. We looked forward to the backpacker's ritual of a foot soak and face wash. As we made our way down, the sun rose higher. With the absence of a tree cover, the heat and dryness worked themselves on me. Need more water! "We've entered the dry West," I thought as we passed prickly pear cactus and yucca plants.

Reaching the South Platte at about 11:00, Segment 1 was now behind us. Crossing the dusty county road, a footbridge led us to shady spots on the opposite bank. Officially designated as the

Gudy Gaskill bridge, it was named after the "Mother of the Colorado Trail." Like all U.S. hiking trails, the Colorado Trail didn't just magically appear. The essence, indeed the very existence, of all such trails stems from visionary and dedicated pioneers who "blazed" the trail into reality. If Myron Avery was the driving force behind the AT's successful construction and completion, Gudy Gaskill is the Myron Avery of the Colorado Trail. No one person accomplishes 100% of all tasks, but Gudy's personal involvement and leadership—marshaling the resources for route planning, dealing with the Forest Service and other landowners, actual trail construction, publicity and community outreach—was critical to the Colorado Trail's very being. Gudy also pioneered as the first woman president of the Colorado Mountain Club. Her accomplishments led to her induction into the Colorado Women's Hall of Fame. Still active in the Colorado Trail Foundation, Gudy wrote the guidebook's foreword plus tips on highlights to look for in each of the trail's 28 segments.

Revising our original plans, we decided not to stay here for the night. Instead, we would rest for a few hours before trying to make it another five miles to Chair Rocks where the guidebook told of "good campsites" awaiting us. The 11.5 miles of the upcoming Segment 2 were entirely devoid of water. We also noticed from the signs that camping was prohibited by the Platte, a little detail in the guidebook that we had overlooked.

For the first of many times on the hike, it was time to replenish our water bottles. Despite the Platte's inviting, crystal-clear appearance, we purified our water using Aqua Mira drops, a solution that many backpackers employ because the drops are highly concentrated and thus don't occupy space or weight in the backpack. Some hikers use filters, some don't treat their water at all, chancing that they won't come up with any waterborne illnesses caused by giardia or any other microorganisms. For the hike's duration, we never failed to treat the water we drew, whether from clear, pristine-looking streams or virtual mudholes where the water's color matched the dirt.

The Platte also served as our wash basin prior to dinner. Now "washing" doesn't involve the use of soap, sponges, or any other aids. We simply waded and splashed in the refreshing *aqua,* savoring the sensation of feeling the accumulated dust wash off of our legs, feet, arms,

South Platte River flows swift and clear.

and face. After cooking hot dinners, we prepared to snooze until dark clouds and distant thunder closed in. Securing the packs with our waterproof covers under the trees, we re-crossed the footbridge and stayed in the overhang of a locked restroom until the storm passed. Said storm featured much wind, lightning, thunder—but not much rain.

Resuming the hike at 2:25 pm, we began hiking steadily uphill through the open burnt-out forest. The initial ascent was bearable but the remainder was a series of rolling ups and downs in the stark environment. Fortunately a cloud cover prevented us from burning too badly. We knew that this entire segment was treeless due to a destructive fire decades ago.

Two frustrating aspects to this ascent: (1) it was rolling up and down, so we were going uphill more than I expected, and (2) much of the trail was in a trench surrounded by gravel-type dirt and loose rocks, making it easy to slip. Regarding the former, this is the problem when excessively relying upon, or more accurately, not diligently studying, the elevation profiles. You see the left-to-right line with little upward movement so you think the trail won't go up

32

and down much. And as you hike, you see that you were wrong. Actually, it's more accurate to substitute "I" instead of "you." For me, when reality renders mental expectations erroneous, the effect is also physical. Undertaking a 1,000' climb over one mile is easier physically when I expect it, when I know it's coming. For the uninitiated, a "1,000' climb" refers to the vertical elevation gained. A 1,000' ladder straight-up gains 1,000' vertically. For backpackers, 1,000' of elevation gained in one trail mile is the rule-of-thumb for steepness. If that doesn't sound steep, I'd be pleased to recommend some slopes for you to hike and see for yourselves!

I've come up with a term to describe this phenomenon: Cookerhiker's First Principle of Erroneous Expectations or PEE (as opposed to pee which hikers do frequently provided they've drunk sufficient water). Another way of putting it: given two uphill stretches of equal elevation gained per mile, the one you expected is easier physically than the one you didn't. When it's a surprise, the ascent is harder. Of course, you also have to factor in time of day, overall miles for the day, did you get a good night's sleep, etc., etc. Why should it be that way? I don't know, but I understand it when many hikers assert that preparing for long-distance hiking is as much mental as physical.

So the cumulative effect of hours and miles was getting to me as I fell behind Northern Harrier. We had hoped to hike five miles from the South Platte but by mutual agreement, we stopped short in an open-air camping area, pitched our tents, and enjoyed the breeze and dry atmosphere.

It was hard to conserve water on such a hot, dry, afternoon hike, but given the lack of water on this entire segment and with another 6-7 miles tomorrow, I had brought an extra liter, giving me three in my backpack (normally, I carried no more than two at a time). Drinking one on the afternoon hike still gave me two full liters for the next day: one for my breakfast meal, the other for the morning hike.

33

Breezes at the campsite were delightful. With the arid atmosphere, I expected to sleep well. But the night was still not very cold, meaning my bag was zipped open and my face sweated slightly. We were both surprised since we thought western hiking at elevations already exceeding the highest point in the East would at least bring us cool nights. I thought that this dry campsite would be noticeably cooler but perspiration still slightly bathed my face when we arose at 5:00 am.

We hit the trail at 6:40. These early starts are the best conditions for hiking, especially in this treeless domain. The morning ups and downs over rolling, still-open terrain again weren't too tough. Consequently, we made good time reaching the county road where our first mail drop awaited us at a general store *cum* post office in the small community of Buffalo Creek, three miles down the blacktop. Now our first hitchhiking opportunity had arrived and we struck out! A hot road walk on unforgiving asphalt ensued as we hoofed it all the way to the store, a tiring and discouraging (for me) walk, even though it was all downhill.

The general store was equally discouraging—an ugly, cinder block building with no shade or porch and dimly lit inside where I could barely see the sparsely-stocked shelves. The woman who greeted us was friendly but she departed when the postmistress arrived. To put it mildly, her cold indifference did not present a welcome persona. Northern Harrier wanted to mail some surplus gear home and politely asked for a box. "I don't know," was her attempt at a response. After we pointed out all the empty boxes strewn about, she mumbled for us to help ourselves. Perhaps she was having a bad day. The store had neither drinking water nor a pay phone (as expected, no cell phone service in this "town") and she couldn't tell us where to find such. An altogether dreary scenario; we fervently hoped the lack of a hitched ride and the atmosphere in this place wasn't a harbinger of our off-trail experience for the rest of the hike.

It wasn't. Things turned up as we were sorting and re-packing outside. A young guy with a dog came by, struck up a conversation, and offered a ride back to the trailhead. Because he was basically living out of his car, we couldn't fit in together with our packs so he made two trips. He was recently homeless and could use our proffered gas money so things worked out. Northern Harrier went first. My turn found me wedging the pack in the back seat with Woodstock the dog while navigating the junk in the front seat to place my legs somewhere. Meanwhile, Woodstock decided he'd like to chew on my trekking poles after finding my ear less palatable. *Deja vu!* This experience reminded me of a time in Connecticut during a point-to-point day-hike on the AT. Scores of cars driven by prosperous-looking upper- and middle-class people of presumably good character passed the hitchhiker (me) for more than an hour. Finally, a young homeless guy with a dog and living out of his car picked me up.

During the ride, our Trail Angel showed me a photo of a vase in his possession that was worth thousands of dollars—or so he hoped, based on preliminary internet research. His aspirations would be realized or dashed in less than a week when he would obtain an appraisal. I hoped it worked out and told him so, wishing him well as I paid him $10 for gas.

On the way up the road, we stopped at a Forest Service office to replenish our water. Now it's not like this stop delayed our hike in any measurable way, but one would think that we could have filled our bottles beforehand from a fire station adjacent to the trailhead. Northern Harrier had circled it and reported no water spigots, faucets, pumps, or anything else from which to procure basic trail libation. No water at a fire station? Really?

Back at the trailhead at 11:45, we were ready to start Segment 3 after eating lunch at a Forest Service picnic ground. We encountered our first fellow backpacker; thus far everyone we met was on mountain bikes. Zero-Zero (his trail name) told us he was totally blind. He normally hikes with a companion but his hiking partner left him, hence his decision to terminate his hike. He'd hiked the AT and PCT so he harbored hopes of attaining the Triple Crown by hiking the CDT someday. His friend Dee, who came to pick him up, offered to call Charlene, Northern Harrier's wife, when she reached an area with cell phone service to assure her we were still alive and well, a gesture which greatly relieved him.

Here it was only our third day and twice in less than a one hour period, we were recipients of Trail Magic provided by Trail Angels. What? When people do good things for hikers, especially when the acts are unexpected, unplanned, spontaneous, arising from circumstances, from being at the right place at the right time—the givers are Trail Angels and the act is Trail Magic. The homeless guy didn't go out looking to do good deeds. He met us, we talked, and his offer of assistance was generated. We all know this kind of serendipity occurs in life as well and is not limited to hikers on trails.

In recent years, the term "Trail Magic" has been misused in a reductionist way to be regarded as one-and-the-same with well-organized and publicized "hiker feeds," and with leaving coolers of food and drinks in the woods where, if not tended to every day, they inevitably cause litter. But the best Trail Magic I've received is real "magic" like the time I lost the tip of my hiking pole, and a hiker behind me a half-hour later happened to see it sticking in the mud. Or back in 1980 when I lost a camera hiking in Vermont, convinced myself it was gone for good, and celebrated my good fortune when it was returned after posting a lost-and-found notice. So on this day, we had received the first of what turned out to be many instances of *bona fide* Trail Magic.

For me, there was nothing magical about the rest of the day's hike. Our intent was to hike five more miles to Tramway Creek but we heard from Zero-Zero that it was dry. It looked like we'd have to hike beyond it until we reached suitable water. We covered the first few miles in good order but then I hit a wall, especially dragging on what were very modest ascents. Our progress slowed considerably. I felt guilty because Northern Harrier was going strong and if I was my usual self, we could have made it to Buffalo Creek (the creek, not the town) at 7.7 miles. But I was too weak. As it turned out, Tramway Creek had sufficient water along with decent campsites, so we made it our night's abode. Now Zero-Zero told us this creek was dry. Wouldn't a blind man actually remember things like this better than Northern Harrier or me? I'll bet he could have found water at that fire station!

Grateful for ending the day's hike, my issue was vexing; just

Large succulent greets us in dry section.

what is the problem? I was still convinced elevation (we went over 8,000' today) because of my heavier-than-normal breathing, even after reaching camp. It was very reminiscent of the second day of my 2006 John Muir Trail hike when I hit a similar wall. Northern Harrier blamed conditioning or lack thereof with which I didn't agree. It wasn't a sense of pride, ego, or shame, but rather I liked to think I knew my body well enough to diagnose this problem. Northern Harrier also raised the very sensible point that we weren't eating enough at breaks. And what about the sun and heat? The road walk did me in. Also, I wasn't peeing despite consuming copious quantities of water fortified with powdered electrolytes. At the Buffalo Creek general store, the bottles of iced tea and vitawater that I had downed apparently didn't help me avoid dehydration. It was pretty obvious by now that to this point, the hike was a jolt to my body. Equally obvious was that tomorrow would be the make/break day as we'd continue to ascend to even higher elevations.

Tents set up, we were preparing dinner when the thunder and lightning intensified. I had eaten most of mine when the rain started at 5:00 pm. Retreating to the tent, I re-emerged in 25 minutes to finish the lukewarm hot chocolate and wash dishes. I didn't hear any more thunder, but sprinkles still fell from the trees as I drifted off to sleep before 7:30, knowing that at least in Colorado we could count on dry mornings.

* * * * *

AND THE MORNING WAS "dry" in that no rain was falling in the still-darkness at 5:00 am when we stirred. My tent was still wet from yesterday's rain; all night long, the sounds of drops falling from the trees reminded me of our wet atmosphere. Entombed in the nylon cocoon, you always wonder: is it raining more or are those just drops blowing down from the trees in this heavily-wooded site? You hope for the latter, you expect it on Colorado mornings.

Considering how weak I felt yesterday afternoon, I had trepidations about our (my) ability to get very far today. Barely at 8,000' now, today's plan called for ascending to the 10,000' level for the first time on this, our fourth day. Northern Harrier suggested taking frequent breaks, along with making sure we gobbled sufficient trail mix at said breaks. At least the early start afforded us plenty of time.

We found ourselves in deep forest most of the day, a dry forest in contrast to the lush foliage of our first day-and-a-half. A fairly easy stretch led us to Buffalo Creek, at 7,364' our lowest point of the day. The last five miles of Segment 3 entailed a 900' ascent which we handled with little difficulty. So far, so good.

38

Approaching a Forest Service road, a trailhead parking lot divided Segments 3 and 4. We met three hikers who were about to drive off, ending their hike at Segment 4.

"Would you like some water? We have a lot and we're about to leave."

"Thanks—I'll take it."

"We got it at that fire station back at the last road."

Northern Harrier's ears perked up: "I never found the water there."

"It was a faucet on the side of the building."

Oh well—let's hope we don't miss any more water sources, we told ourselves.

We also met three other guys hiking in the same direction as us but car trouble forced an alteration of their plans. So far we hadn't met any fellow thru-hikers, northbound or southbound.

Today's test came after lunch with a 2,000' ascent. The first 1,000' featured an initially steep portion that became more manageable as the trail leveled off. The second 1,000' was much tougher—steep most of the way through dense forest, away from the old logging road we had initially followed. I felt the strain as the day and the miles wore on, but I was ecstatic because 24 hours ago, I never could have made it to 10,000' which we did while still in the dense forest. I was surprised to find that we weren't near treeline at that elevation. To an easterner, 10K seems so high, it must be alpine, right? Wrong! But that didn't matter. What was important was that I could enjoy the forest without gasping and needing to rest every ten minutes. My prior days' problems must have been elevation-related. Today felt just like any "ordinary" steep ascent; I wasn't breathing abnormally on the hike or in our campsite.

Speaking of the latter, we finally began descending from a high of 10,500' as the trail left the forest for a scenic-looking meadow with grasses and shrubs. We knew that Lost Creek flowed somewhere in the middle and then we found it. Not lost any more!

Racing against a threatening sky, we found a firm, i.e. non-mucky, grassy area near the creek and set up the tents just as the sprinkles started. After 10-15 minutes, the sun emerged and stayed with us for the next two hours, long enough to dry everything from last night's dampness and for us to cook our dinners. We enjoyed a delightful few hours until dark clouds rolled in again.

Only one downside: cows were grazing upstream so we double treated our water with our Aqua Mira solution. The brownish tint caused me to boil my supper water longer than usual. "Hiker midnight" was marked with another early bedtime. We expected to have a brighter campground in the morning with the open setting.

Around 10:00 pm, the thunderstorms began in earnest. For nearly an hour, heavy rain pelted our tents. Aside from a small wet spot near my feet, I was warm and dry. And for the first night on this trek, we had a colder night worthy of the Rocky Mountains. We should at 10,000'! Snuggling in my winter sleeping bag, it was refreshing to not experience a sweaty face.

Camping in the broad Lost Creek Meadow.

So how cold was it? Like most backpackers who sleep in tents, my shelter features two layers: the tent proper which is thin and "breathable," and a waterproof cover referred to as a fly. The next morning, water on my tent fly from the night's rain had frosted over. The fly was stiff despite all the shaking I could muster. And notwithstanding my prediction, it was the other side of the meadow, not ours, that basked in the morning sun, a sun whose later arrival each morning was noticeable as we continued to rise at 5:00 am.

Unlike my usual morning routine where I pack everything up and save breakfast for last, I left the tent standing while preparing and eating breakfast, hoping the tent fly would thaw at least partially. But it didn't. Hoping to still fit both pieces into the tent bag (the sack used for carrying them), I began stuffing the tent into the bag but the fly was still too stiff and nonpliable. I resorted to wrapping it with my (wet) groundcloth and tying it near the bottom of the pack where my tent usually rides. The tent now sat on top. Meanwhile, my hands, which are very susceptible to frostbite, were virtually nonfunctional.

We were still off at a good hour for what became a dispiriting five miles through the meadow. The "dispiriting" aspect was that the entire meadow was a cow pasture, a factoid not mentioned in the guidebook. In addition to avoiding frequent cow patties, we shared the meadow and the trail with literally hundreds of cows. Despite their deferential docility, our experience was anything but fun as we hiked along a gradually-upward grade. Later on in the hike when we talked to a fellow trail user and I expressed frustration with this bovine atmosphere, the listener responded, "We have multiple use on these [National Forest] lands...," to which I replied, "So do we back east, but our multiple use is logging and sometimes mining, not grazing on this scale." It's quite apparent that "multiple use" on public lands in the west encompasses a greater range (no pun intended!) of said "uses" than the eastern National Forests.

After what seemed an interminable time, the trail finally left the meadow and proceeded through a grove of young aspens in a section where evidently a fire had cleared the forest. We began descending to the end of Segment 4. Entering Segment 5, we had managed to average a segment each day but that would change when we encountered the 32-mile Segment 6.

Today's 15 miles were much easier than yesterday's 15 miles when our ascents gained at least 3,000'. I was gratified because I was more tired today and would have had difficulty with an ascent of this magnitude again. Of course, not all 3,000' ascents are alike. Obviously, 3,000' hiked in 4-5 miles is much tougher and steeper than the same elevation change over 10 miles. Yesterday's climb was of medium difficulty in that portions were gradual while others, particularly the last 1,000', were noticeably steeper. To a degree, ascents occurring later in the day are more taxing whether steep, gradual, or something in-between. Fatigue can set in after hiking mostly uphill for 10-12 miles, the quad muscles can ache, and any intervening descents may hurt the knees. I've also already found on this hike, as my previous long hikes, that the effect of long ascents is day-to-day, depending on the cumulative impact of previous day's ups and downs, whether I slept well the previous night, my nourishment at meals, and other factors that I can't seem to pinpoint.

In any case, it's not something to dwell incessantly on since we faced many lengthy ascents coming up as we approached the much-anticipated alpine areas. And of course, we'd become stronger as the days progressed and as our fitness increased from the constant, steady workout from each day's hike.

A steady and faster-than-expected pace covering the last 7.5 miles to Rock Creek ended the hiking day for us at 2:30 pm. While mid-afternoon may seem like an early time to quit, we reasoned that 15 miles constituted a more-than-adequate day. More importantly, Rock Creek was a logical place to camp with nice sites under some tree cover and a good water source.

And then there's the Rocky Mountain weather. True to form, thunderheads were upon us along with intervals of blue sky. I had hoped to further dry my tent fly and groundcloth but the sprinkles were frequent enough to erect the tent and secure everything. Sprinkles stopped, sun emerged (along with mosquitoes), so I washed my feet and legs in the creek while thunder continued to roll in the distance. Already we'd learned how hard it is to predict exactly when and how much actual rain will fall. The daily occurrence of thunder, winds, perhaps lightning, and gray skies of various hues do not always translate into precipitation, at least not on us. We were convinced that erecting our tents and stuffing everything inside had warded off the rain. It's the same syndrome that says when hiking, mounting one's waterproof cover on the backpack at the first hint of rain will ensure that said rain never transpires.

We had arrived when the sky was predominantly gray, evincing a few shades of blue and black. This seemed to be the pattern thus far on the hike, so it behooved us to continue our 6 am starts and reach camp by no later than mid-afternoon. We couldn't always count on such exquisite timing with our hiking pace and desired camping locales *vis-a-vis* weather patterns but so far, things worked.

We cooked early dinners, washed in the creek some more, talked about tomorrow's plans, and retired to our tents by 6:30 for an early "hiker midnight."

And one more tidbit to cap the day: for the first time on this hike, we didn't meet or even see a soul—hiker, biker, horse rider, no one else passed us today. We never crossed a road (the segment division was a few hundred feet from a dirt access road upon which no one was visible). From our campsite, we saw signs of civilization down the hollow—a barn and maybe a vehicle. But not a person. I had anticipated that we'd experience such days perhaps in 2-3 weeks, when Denver was well behind us as we entered segments far from roads and Front Range settlements. I did not expect that a day this early in the hike would be bereft of people. Of course there were all those cows! I guess that's civilization of a sort.

The next day's ambitious plan called for hiking to Jefferson Creek where we would camp for the night. This would place us in good position for the following morning to hike up to Georgia Pass where we would finally rise above treeline into the alpine country. Our customary early morning start would help us avoid the commonplace thunderstorms whose frequency, not to say intensity, increased at higher elevations.

But first things first: upon reaching the highway at Kenosha Pass today, we would also need to hitch rides, to and from, the small crossroads hamlet of Jefferson for our second maildrop of supplies. Our destination was a general store housing a post office.

Ready to start by 6:20 am, Northern Harrier motioned for me to go first.

"Are you sure? I think you should lead."

"Nope—go ahead."

Describing our hiking paces is not a simple subject. Overall, Northern Harrier is a stronger hiker because he's more athletic, a result of running most of his life, including marathons until recently. He points out that I have stronger legs, which is true. The only "natural" physical trait I possess is strong calf muscles. But I maintain that aerobic fitness is the single most important element leading to a successful and enjoyable hike; in this respect, he's in "better shape" and, consequently, usually hikes ahead. His long legs also translate into longer strides.

There are two purported exceptions: (1) I'm allegedly stronger on the ascents; and (2) I'm noticeably stronger in the first hour or so in the morning. Regarding (1), reality—not just on this hike but the next-longest hike we did together (Vermont's Long Trail)—dictates that before long into a hike, he's effectively stronger than me over all terrains: uphill, downhill, level, rocks, whatever. As to (2), this stereotype is generally accurate. Unless I've had a very poor night's sleep, I am strong "out-of-the-box" and really enjoy, if not crave, hiking uphill first thing in the morning. While strong starts evoke a good feeling, I wish I could "even it out" over the course of the day, especially those days where I'm beat by mid-afternoon. But it's not like that every day. Strange...

So the latter consideration is why he said "Go ahead" and for this morning at least, he was dead-on. Feeling very strong, I led the way for the entire stretch to the pass while Northern Harrier remarked about how vigorous a pace I was setting. The Trail brought us up along an open ridge where for most of the morning's 7.8 miles, we enjoyed gorgeous vistas of the high mountains ahead marking the Continental Divide. Continuous colorful wildflowers of every

Approaching Kenosha Pass, the snow-covered high peaks loom ahead.

hue were our trailside entertainment. Some we were familiar with such as Indian paintbrush, wild geraniums, a variant of sunflower, and the ever-present asters, but many were unknown to us. This morning, for the first time, I felt like I was hiking in Colorado. The peaks of the now-closer high mountains stared at us. Sweeping high-elevation valleys proclaimed that yes, we were in the Rocky Mountains.

We hiked those 7.8 miles in 3 hours, 10 minutes, a good pace considering that the ascents' gross total exceeded 1,000'. At Kenosha Pass, the next issue was hitching a ride, hoping for better luck than our first attempt on Day 3. Score! After 15 minutes, along came a Trail Angel who not only drove us the 4.5 miles to Jefferson, but also returned us to the pass. He was a former Colorado Trail thru-hiker who said he wanted to "give back"—this was his way of doing so. Unlike Buffalo Creek, the women staffing the Jefferson general store/post office were very friendly. We picked up our maildrops, incorporated their contents into our packs, bought sandwiches and drinks, headed back to the pass courtesy of our Trail Angel, and strolled into the Forest Service campground marking the start of Segment 6. The nice host allowed us to use the picnic tables even though it was technically not a picnic ground. Enjoying a leisurely lunch, we gazed ahead at the beckoning alpine country.

Reaching 12K — Kenosha Pass to Tennessee Pass

"The spectacular alpine setting was capped in the foreground by the massive-looking Mt. Guyot, surrounded by tundra grass, flowers, and a few snow patches."
Day 7 — July 30, 2011

T HINGS HAD GONE WELL SO FAR with 68 miles under our belts, er, boots. Acclimation to high altitudes no longer appeared to be an issue. No serious aches, pains, etc. and most importantly, no blisters. We had already enjoyed a variety of terrain in the form of moist deciduous forests, dry forests of lodgepole pines, open arid areas affording distant views, wildflowers galore, and sparkling creeks frequent enough that water wasn't a concern. Even the Lost Creek meadow was scenic, notwithstanding the cows and the muck they fostered. And now on July 29, our sixth day of hiking, we were about to head to the glorious high alpine country.

It was 11:30 am when we hoisted our packs and resumed the trek onto the 32-mile Segment 6 (the longest of the Colorado Trail's 28 segments), which would take us over the high mountains and deposit us in our first real town stop, the resort community of Breckenridge. For the mere six miles to our night's destination of Jefferson Creek, we planned on taking about four hours, a leisurely pace necessitated by our heavier packs and more substantial-than-average lunch. But then we delayed ourselves by talking to people we met.

After passing four mountain bikers (an activity with absolutely no appeal to me, but I'm in awe of those who partake), we met two women day-hikers at the top of the first ridge. They shared their

knowledge of the wildflowers we had seen, showing descriptions and photos in their excellent guidebook. They also expressed admiration for our ambition of thru-hiking the entire Colorado Trail, a sentiment we'd hear often throughout the remainder of the hike.

A Mariposa Lilly graces the corridor.

Next was a Dutch man in his 20s named Marco, about to enter a mountain bike race for which he was training and acclimating. Our conversation reminded us that it was the time of year when mountain bikers, road bikers, horse riders, day-hikers, runners, and backpackers all converge on the Rocky Mountains for their recreational pursuits, some of which were sponsored events. And we finally met a Colorado Trail thru-hiker: a young, early 20ish woman named Elly who hiked much faster than us (an observation, not a judgement). She had seen our footprints and figured, correctly, that she'd catch us. Since she skipped Segments 1 and 2, Elly was technically not a thru-hiker, but she did intend to hike all the way to Durango. Shortly afterward, we met Jeff, our first northbound thru-hiker. We appreciated Jeff's many pointers on what to expect as we forged ahead.

All told, we probably spent close to an hour on these encounters and it cost us as the clouds over head became darker. After a final brief conversation with an Illinois couple near Guernsey Creek, we hustled along but didn't avoid our first rain while actually hiking. Thus far, all of the rain had occurred after we had stopped for the day and set up our tents.

So wasn't it time for some Trail Magic? No kidding—some inadvertent Trail Angels emerged. Just as the rain had become hail bouncing off our bodies and bringing colder temperatures, we heard voices and noticed some people on the right side with tents and canopies. "Come on up!" they beckoned. And for the next 15 minutes, we had a dry spot along with pleasant conversation with two families including kids of various ages and two dogs. We were at a junction with a Forest Service road on which they had driven and were camping roadside for a few days. It's nice that the Forest Service allows dispersed camping so that these families had a free campsite reasonably close to Jefferson Lake where they had enjoyed a swim.

When the precipitation stopped, we moved on. Just as we arrived at Jefferson Creek, the rain picked up again but only briefly. At the creek, a Forest Service sign appeared to prohibit camping in the "Jefferson Creek area" but we crossed the creek and found spots among trees in a dense evergreen forest. The guidebook did not indicate any camping prohibition here.

The sun's late afternoon re-emergence allowed us to dry some things in those few places where the rays penetrated the tree cover, a setting which soon rendered the campsite very dark. Today's only downside was mosquitoes—they pretty much controlled the environment, which is why I wrote my journal ensconced in the tent in broad daylight. Outside, Northern Harrier was fixing dinner, but most of what I heard was him slapping the mosquitoes! At my turn, I cooked and ate while standing up and walking around to minimize the blood loss. The little bloodsuckers also besieged us in the morning.

Another warm night passed even though we were residing at nearly 10,000' Unbelievable! The previous evening, I had talked to a mountain biker who informed us that the weekend forecast was dry and hot. And a weekend in July meant that we'd have company on the trail tomorrow going up to Georgia Pass. I just hoped that the next day's planned campsite at the North Fork of the Swan River wasn't too crowded or noisy, especially considering its accessibility via a road. At least the map indicated that it wasn't a paved highway, but more likely a gravel or even a four-wheel-drive vehicle dirt road.

* * * * *

TODAY, JULY 30, WAS THE BIG DAY, rising up to nearly the 12,000' level with our first extensive above-treeline hiking as we approached Georgia Pass. Our dark and damp campsite made things more difficult to work at our accustomed speed, but we were still on the uphill trek by 6:25 am. Our 1,900' ascent to the pass was spread out over six miles but it seemed like much of the eleva-

Emerging from treeline near Georgia Pass.

tion gain was in the first mile-and-a-half or so. Also, with the exception of one outstanding vista after about a mile, we hiked through thick forest for at least four miles. The setting of statuesque spruce and fir trees wearing their emerald-green needles was delightful in itself but I kept wondering: when do we emerge from treeline?

We began seeing views on our left as the trees thinned out before finally leaving them for good and emerging into the open. A

50

spectacular alpine setting unfolded before our eyes, capped in the foreground by the massive-looking Mt. Guyot, surrounded by tundra grass, flowers, and a few snow patches. And it was another incredibly warm day. I couldn't believe we were at nearly 12,000' in the first half of the morning with temperatures around 70-75 degrees. Only a slight breeze blew, meaning the omnipresent mosquitoes were still a nuisance.

Once in the open, we trod more uphill to reach the pass. For the first time in a few days, I felt slightly affected by the elevation but not as severely as Day 3. And unlike that day, in this setting our eyes and other senses enjoyed the alpine splendor. After reaching the Continental Divide Trail intersection, we continued up to the (unmarked) high point of the pass at 11,874'. The Colorado Trail would henceforth coincide with the CDT for the next 99 miles. We plopped down on some rocks slightly below the top, basked in the sun,

The Continental Divide Trail joins the Colorado Trail atop Georgia Pass.

still swatted mosquitoes, and ate an early lunch while gazing at Mt. Guyot. "Must be a 14er" we thought, but a perusal of the guidebook revealed that our assumption that Mt. Guyot's elevation topped 14,000' was mistaken. "Sure is different from the 'other' Mt. Guyots." We knew of two through which the AT passes: one in the Great Smoky Mountains of Tennessee, one in the White Mountains of New Hampshire. The former tops 6,000', the latter over 4,500'. By eastern standards, quite impressive but their combined elevation falls well short of the Rockies' Mt. Guyot's 13,370'. This contrast certainly puts Colorado in perspective!

A few mountain bikers came by from whom we learned of a riding event sponsored by the cycling company Yeti. Over 100 bikers started from Kenosha Pass at 9:00 this morning heading south on the trail, i.e. towards us. So, for most of the way until reaching our campsite, we stayed alert to the bikers' presence, stepping aside when we heard the bikes and/or riders approaching from behind. In one stretch while still above treeline, we sat by the side watching about 20-30 riders speed by within a ten minute span. For a while, Northern Harrier was keeping count as in "You're the 16th rider so far" or "Congratulations—you're the first woman." Most of the cyclists were polite and friendly, with a few even wishing us good luck on our thru-hike.

Later on we talked to some riders after the race was over—all good conversation. Any tension or disparagement between hikers and bikers was not discernible. It's worth noting that not once did we encounter bikers in Wilderness Areas where they are forbidden, a testimony to the cyclists' "good citizenship" and ethic of environmental stewardship. And I sensed a healthy mutual admiration for the others' feats. For my part, mountain biking seems much more arduous, with the tough uphill pulls challenging one's stamina and the steep descents being outright dangerous. The rocky stretches on both ups and downs bounce your body around, and I'm not certain that the best shock absorbers improve the comfort of the ride any more than marginally. On the other hand, several cyclists expressed awe that we were hiking 480 miles carrying heavy packs and dealing with the (routine to us) matters of setting up camps, cooking, finding water, having to re-supply, and going days without showers. The dialog was a joy, today and later in the hike right up to our last day.

I found myself hungry shortly after lunch. Not unexpected; after seven days on the trail, my appetite was accelerating. I had developed "thru-hiker appetite," little surprise considering that our diet over the past week was limited in both variety and caloric content. Breakfast always consisted of oatmeal and hot chocolate. Lunch was cheese and trail mix of nuts and dried fruits whereas dinners always combined a starchy grain (rice, pasta, bulgur wheat, couscous) with a reconstituted sauce mix, usually cheese or pesto. Fare like this makes for a lighter and less bulky load in the pack but over time, the enormous amount of calories burned from hiking 13 or more miles daily over mountainous terrain takes its toll. The hunger pangs arrive faster and more frequently. And then there's the sheer monotony of this homogenous diet with its dearth of fresh meats, fruits, vegetables, breads, etc. Arriving in Breckenridge tomorrow would grant us an opportunity to engage in shameless gluttony to compensate for all those lost calories! Both of us looked forward with eager anticipation to enjoying a bed, shower, and "real" food. Breckenridge was also a milestone of sorts in that we would pass the 100-mile mark.

The final descent to the North Fork of Swan Creek was up-and-down—so what else is new? Some very rocky stretches reminded me of Northern New England and again, I thought of how the mountain bikers either bounce over them or steer adroitly to dodge the more egregious ones while avoiding collisions with trees of the increasingly denser forest. Considering our seemingly slow pace in this rock-strewn terrain, I was surprised when we pulled in to the camping area at 3:45 pm. Decent campsites were plentiful and spread out, resulting in less-crowded conditions than I anticipated. We chose a site near the creek, perfect except for again being besieged by mosquitoes. Most of our fellow campers appeared to be lodged here as a base for their day hiking or mountain biking.

Towards evening as our "hiker midnight" drew nigh, we waved to three arriving hikers with full backpacks as they passed nearby and selected their sites. Early the next morning, we saw them again as they had built a campfire and made breakfast. We chatted briefly and bade them goodbye a few minutes after 6:00 am—our earliest start to date.

Contrary to our normal first-of-the-day pattern, Northern Harrier took the lead as we began the initial ascent. I thought I felt pretty strong but he was on a mission, striding up the steep slope as if it was flat! Was he motivated by today's town stop? No way could I keep up with him until he slowed down a bit after the terrain leveled off somewhat.

A morning with little mosquito interference was a pleasure on this beautiful day. Ahead of us rose Tenmile Range whose heights rose over 13,000'. A fabulous sight greeted us as we gazed at the strip of pure white snow illuminated by the early morning alpenglow along the top of this steep range. What we looked at in the

Columbine, the state flower of Colorado, flourished above treeline.

distance comprised tomorrow's hike, stretched out clearly for us.

Underfoot, today may have been the best day yet for wildflowers; they were profuse and we frequently stopped to take pho-

54

tos of those we hadn't captured yet. Some such pictures included mountains as a backdrop, making an ideal postcard scene. Fields of columbine, the state flower, were supplemented by harebells, blue flax, orange sneezeweed, and asters. Others making their first appearance included lupines and fireweed.

My best intents at describing the wondrous beauty of the colors fall short. Does bright blue—not pale blue, not bluish purple, but blue with the intensity of an autumn sky—really complement yellow with an orange tint? Likely not in human-constructed works. But place blue flax next to orange sneezeweed, add an array of other grasses, flowers, evergreen trees looming behind, and snow-

Blue flax complements orange sneezeweed

capped Rocky Mountains in the background and you have perfection. Formal gardens are beautiful in their own way but they can't approach Nature's mixing and matching. Writer and social activist Victor Hugo stated it well when he wrote, "What would be ugly in a garden constitutes beauty in a mountain."

We met only a few mountain bikers this morning, but many more in the afternoon. Aside from a Boy Scout troop out for a few days, we saw no hikers or backpackers. After a week, we still hadn't met any "true" Colorado Trail southbound thru-hikers, that is, hikers going the entire 482-mile route in one trip.

After that difficult 1,000' ascent up fom the campsite, we enjoyed walking along the ridge where the trail alternated between spruces and firs along with dead lodgepole pines, victims of the pine bark beetle. Many of the pines were recently cut down, a move which will help the forest regenerate. From a conversation with two mountain bikers, we learned some facts about Breckenridge, the trail, and the overall ecosystem through which we passed. They also told us about the bus system in Summit County connecting Breckenridge, Frisco, Copper Mountain, and Dillon. Taking advantage of this rare instance of public transportation, we planned a "slackpack" day-hike tomorrow covering the 15 miles over the Tenmile Range and past the resort of Copper Mountain.

After two intervening ascents, our final descent to Breckenridge took us down steep slopes through a suburban-type neighborhood and to Colorado Rt. 9. Here the guidebook failed us by stating that the trailhead (and endpoint of Segment 6) was reached by crossing Rt. 9 and walking a half-mile to the right along a paved bike trail (upon which numerous Sunday riders were cycling). The bus stop was also supposed to be in this direction. Shortly after turning onto the bike trail, I noticed a parking lot, but it was much less than a half-mile so we continued on. After trooping on for about a mile (good half-hour at least), we realized our, and the book's, mistake.

Turning around, walking back in drizzle, passing the parking lot which was the true segment terminus and the start of the next day's hike, we found the bus stop. Upon arriving in downtown Breckenridge, we solicited directions to the Fireside Inn from a couple on the bus and settled in.

Item #1 on our agenda was the first shower in a week. I'm not sure there's a way to quantify the "appreciation score" of a hot shower but I submit that the sensation of hot water flowing down your body and literally watching, as well as feeling, seven days worth of dust, sweat, and grime all loosening from the body and down the drain ranks pretty high. A shower after a (single) day of hard physical labor (e.g. yard work or home repairs) or one after a vigorous workout at a gym certainly feels refreshing, as does the morning shower before going to work. But in all of these circumstances, the presence of the high-pressure hot *agua* is taken for granted as part of one's daily routine. On the trail, we also follow a daily routine; it's just a tad different from "normal," at least what passes for normal in 21st Century America. A shower feels like a luxury not afforded to us every day. And that's precisely the situation.

Bodies cleaned and refreshed (and bereft of odors!), we next retrieved our maildrops which had safely arrived at the Inn. The boxes may have contained the "same old, same old" foodstuffs but there's something pleasurable about opening the packages, confirming that yes, we have provisions for the next phase. Now I know what's in the box—after all, I packed it. That, however, doesn't completely dispel the sensation similar to opening a Christmas or birthday present: the feeling of anticipation as the packing tape is unraveled and the box contents revealed. Will there be a surprise treat inside? Of course not, so why do I think that way? Irrational, I know, but does it really matter? And along the lines of the "shower appreciation" score, I probably appreciate seeing the grains, dried sauce mixes, oatmeal mix, hot chocolate, etc. more in these circumstances than the feeling I have procuring food of a greater gourmet quality shopping the grocery store at home. These rather drab and frankly boring victuals will be our nourishment for the next several days, so we celebrate their arrival. And speaking of celebrating over the subject of food, we topped off the day with a dinner of burgers and ice cream at one of the many little restaurants in town.

Run by an English couple, Nikki and Andy, the Fireside Inn featured both conventional bed-and-breakfast rooms and dorm-like hostel rooms. Services included doing our laundry and a "hiker box" consisting of someone else's surplus food, supplies, whatever they didn't want to carry anymore. "Someone else" denotes previous hiker guests. It is not uncommon for hikers to realize that the nuts, fruits, granola bars, rice, oatmeal, etc. that they're toting will cover eight meals when they only need six. Or perhaps, they end their hike prematurely for one reason or another. "Hiker boxes" are a win-win outlet for some hikers to dispose of excess provisions to the benefit of those hikers who have run short.

Andy also offered me free fuel canisters, for which I was grateful. In what appeared to be a touristy town catering to the *nouveau riche*, we were very appreciative that the Fireside Inn offered this hostel option. Naturally (ironic use of the adverb!), it was gratifying to sleep in a bed after seven nights in tents on the trail. Next up was tomorrow's slackpack.

So what is a "slackpack?" Apparently the term originated in the early 1980s to describe AT hikers who moved in a leisurely manner, not concerned about making it to the next town or road crossing "in time" or racking up "big miles" every day. They were hiking a "slackened" pace. One of the first "slackpackers" is said to have hiked the AT starting in late February and finishing in late November, making his nine-month trek the longest of all thru-hikers that year. He took his time, enjoyed the trip, and not incidentally, carried a heavy pack. Another multi-time AT thru-hiker acquired the trail name "Yankee Slackpacker" in the mid-1980s because of his heavy pack and slow pace.

Contemporarily, the meaning has shifted almost 180 degrees. Today's "slackpacker" is a backpacker who avails himself of the opportunity to leave the full pack at a hostel, motel, with a friend, etc, and hike a stretch in one day with a light pack/day pack. It's basically a day-hike. This option presupposes some transportation means—shuttles, hitching, or in our case, a public bus system to bring us to and from the trailhead. And while a few "purist" backpackers frown on slackpacking as something less than a "true" hike, we had no hesitation about taking advantage of this opportunity. Nothing changed the fact that we were hiking the entire Colorado Trail in one fell swoop.

So this upcoming Segment 7 almost cries for a slackpack. The distance (14.5 miles) makes for a good day-hike, the bus system is in place, we have a hiker-friendly hostel to return to where our gear is safely stored, and the hike over Tenmile Range features steep terrain and extensive elevation gain—over 3,700'. Thus far there are no "easy" days on the Colorado Trail and even our "slackened" packs would still not guarantee an "easy" day tomorrow. Statistically as measured by elevation gain/loss per mile, Segment 7 is the Colorado Trail's steepest.

Breakfast at a café named Daylight DoNuts provided more than just the namesake as we partook of hearty omelet dishes and other fare. The restaurant opened at 6:00 am, enabling us to catch the 6:45 bus and hit the trail at 7:00, where we faced an immediate uphill. After regaining my trail lungs, my rhythm was set. Although later than our typical starts from campsites thus far, it was early enough to reap the benefits of morning light as the enchanting glow of the sun behind us shone on the peaks of Tenmile Range.

A few up-and-down ridges intervened, but otherwise the trail was straight up with varied grading. The steepest part commenced after the last crossing of Miners Creek, picturesque in its clear, fresh-looking sparkly waters. I didn't look it up, but Northern Harrier said we ascended 700' in four-tenths of a mile. Rather slow going on that part! Once again, the colorful and

Tenmile Range was laced with snow patches.

vibrant flowers were beautiful so we took even more photos. "Will we ever learn them?" I thought. "I should buy a book."

Fortunately, again the weather held up; despite occasional dark clouds, no precipitation materialized as we rose above treeline. Early in the day, we met one biker and one trail runner. After reaching the crest at a point where we could see Breckenridge on the left and the Copper Mountain resort on the right, we met a hiker named Eric coming in our direction. Eric was also slackpacking. Although he was hiking Segment 7 in a northerly direction today, he was thru-hiking the Colorado Trail southbound so it was very likely that our paths would cross again. Eric shared some information on the remainder of the segment ahead.

Impressive wildlife sighting of the day: Northern Harrier spotted a fox sauntering along on the slope below us. Good eyes on his part, considering how well the fox blended in to the landscape. The other piece of fun: for the first time, we traversed close enough to snowfields to romp in them and make snowballs. But we didn't waste energy on a snowball fight!

Our descent was steep in places, but we made good time to Colorado Rt. 91. This road crossing officially ended Segment 7, but we hiked 1.7 more miles to get closer to the heart of the Copper Mountain resort near the point where we could catch the return bus. Copper Mountain was an extensive, sprawling complex with condominiums, shopping malls, a golf course, ski slopes, the infrastructure to support it all—and almost deserted. While billed as a four season resort, it appeared ski season was its prime. It took us a while to figure out where and how to leave the trail to reach one of the bus stops. Meanwhile looking back at Tenmile Range, the dark clouds told us we had escaped a drenching and perhaps a beating from hailstones.

Back in Breckenridge and looking at tomorrow's hike, we decided to not hike all the way to the next high-elevation destinations of Elk Ridge and Kokomo Pass because the bus schedule wouldn't get us on the trail until after 7:00 am. Starting this late meant that afternoon would be upon us by the time we reached the open, above-treeline high point where we'd likely be more vulnerable to afternoon thunderstorms. So instead of any zero (non-hiking) days, we decided to sleep in and take a "nero" (**ne**arly **zero**) day tomorrow. We planned on hiking four miles from the bus stop to camp at Jacque Creek, a point just before the big ascent. We'd then hit the high country the next day (Wednesday, August 3) and reach our next town stop in Leadville on Thursday.

It's not too soon: I could confidently assert I was trail-hardy now. The early days' problems of dehydration, gasping for breath, and fatigue seemed well behind me. On our ninth day of hiking, we were nearly at the one-quarter mark and I felt optimistic about our chances of finishing this trail. One very positive sign: absolutely no foot problems plagued me such as blisters, bruises, sprains, etc. Knees were doing well, no serious falls yet—what could stop us other than being struck by lightning?

* * * * *

EARLY MORNING CLOUDS obscuring the tops of some of the Tenmile Range peaks confirmed that we made the right decision to slackpack yesterday and take our "nero" today. On long hikes, a "zero" day, i.e. a break for a "day off" from hiking is beneficial to rest both body and mind. But I've always preferred "nero" days where you hike a few miles and rest the remainder of the day. The rest can either occur at the end of a short day of hiking or at the beginning of the day in which case you start your short-mileage day's hike later, as we would do in departing Breckenridge.

So I slept in until 7:00 am while Northern Harrier didn't rise until 8:00. After another breakfast at Daylight DoNuts, we packed our stuff and emptied the room. Walking the short distance to the Post Office, I shipped home some clothes, various odds & ends, and my Keen sandals, leaving me with no shoes other than my hiking boots. The sandals gave me lighter and more comfortable shoes to change into at the end of each day's hike, and could also be used for stream fords. In hiker parlance, my Keens served as my "camp shoes." However, it looked like we faced no fords and my hiking boots were comfortable enough. My pack was now lightened by six pounds and I immediately felt the difference.

After lunch in Breckenridge, the buses to Copper Mountain put us on the trail before 2:15 pm. During the bus ride, we talked to an older couple from Oklahoma who spent every summer in Colorado. Smart move! Amidst the confusion of the resort, we managed to find our access trail to the Colorado Trail and hike on.

As expected, most of the hike was uphill (a gain of over 700') in which we gradually put the resort and the din from nearby Interstate 70 traffic behind us. We met a few mountain bikers as we hiked in a slight drizzle with our pack covers on. Our 4:00 arrival at the confluence of two creeks meant that we had reached our destination for the night's camp. Nicer sites were up on a knoll where we enjoyed views and flowers. We expected to see more mountain bikers going our way as part of a race to Durango, the race that Marco, the young Dutchman we had met south of Kenosha Pass, was training for. Some cyclists did indeed pass, mostly not aware of our presence on the knoll, not even when they stopped to refill their water bottles from the creek. But hikers? Nary a one going all the way.

That is, until three backpackers arrived just as we finished our dinner and just as the skies promised imminent rain. We recognized them as the hikers we had briefly met at the Swan Creek campsite before Breckenridge. This time, we had time for conversation with the father, daughter, and daughter's boyfriend. They had recently appropriated trail names for themselves: Rocci, Pocahontas, Stahlberg. Rocci lived in Colorado while the younger two hailed from San Diego. A week-long section-hike would bring them to the Mt. Massive trailhead south of Leadville.

The rain, which began at 6:30, chased me into the tent for the rest of the night. Unlike our experience thus far, it was persistent and unrelenting. For at least three hours, the steady drumbeat became too much for my tent, whose floor was vulnerable to heavy soakers. The bottom of my sleeping bag was wet along with stuff sacks and other things that I'd rather keep dry. My body core remained warm and dry but I didn't sleep well, a factor which I knew would affect my hiking stamina.

Northern Harrier and I arose at 4:50 am, noting another tent down the knoll with a bike parked nearby. First steps commenced at 6:05. Everything was wet—tent, fly, groundcloth, sleeping pad, some clothes. We had heard that a Pacific tropical storm would bring heavy rain in the mountains around this time; it looked like we bore its brunt. But like all mornings on this hike, the sun radiated brightly in an azure sky. At this hour, it was still cool enough to start with two layers so I wore my new windbreaker, a Marmot brand I had purchased shortly before the hike. There's some sense of symmetry in wearing a Marmot windbreaker while hiking in an area inhabited by marmots! The ground, trees, and bushes were all wet and tickled my legs as I brushed past them, but the rapidly-arriving warmth of the emerging sun dried everything in less than two hours.

Faced with an 1,800' ascent spread out over seven miles, we trudged steadily. A few PUDs made the ascent more like 2,500'. For those unaware, "PUD" signifies Pointless Up and Down and describes steep, intervening knobs or hills in which you typically hike straight up and immediately down with no views or other rewards for your effort. PUDs "get in the way" of hiking from point A to point B. I realize that sounds wimpy, and undoubtedly some hikers would say so. PUDs are part of the trail so we are expected to deal with them. In fact, a *hiker* should realize that the very concept of labeling these geographical features as "pointless" is offensive and oxymoronic. Are you a "real" hiker if you complain about PUDs? Celebrate them! John Muir never complained about PUDs. They come with the territory. What are you hiking for—the trip itself or merely the destination? If the latter, why not drive?

Well yes, but it's just human in some of us that as we look forward to scaling a high point, we anticipate the rewards as a trade-off for the attendant stresses and strains of long ascents. Such rewards may include splendid vistas, colorful alpine vegetation, cooler temperatures and breezes, and perhaps changes in ecozones. We have no problem accepting that we're hiking uphill to attain these rewards. But we just want to hike up; we don't want to hike up and then down and then up and then down and then up...

Earlier, I introduced my PEE (Principle of Erroneous Expectations) which states that ascents you did not expect are more difficult physically than those uphills that you know about and anticipate. Many PUDs fall into that category. Northern Harrier can testify that I like hiking uphill, and regard downhills with a mixture of annoyance and dread. Encountering an intervening PUD as part of a long ascent means an undesirable downhill, as well as more uphill than expected, hence my estimate that the 1,800' ascent was really about 2,500'.

To help ameliorate the PEE effect, the guidebook helpfully provides the gross elevation ascent and descent for each segment which for the current Segment 8 was 4,400' of ascent spread out over the segment's 25 miles. One advantage of carrying a GPS (I guess it's an advantage) is that you find out precisely how many feet of elevation that you actually ascended, encompassing PUDs and every little instance where your front foot is placed slightly higher than the back foot. This point was brought home to me the previous winter on a day-hike with some friends on the AT in Western Virginia. My estimate based on the map and guide that we had ascended about 2,000' was belied by the hiker with the GPS announcing that we had gained 3,500'!

And one more thing about PUDs: we who are out here know they're part of hiking in mountains or any terrain that's not pancake flat, but isn't there a curious lack of reference to them in any genre of literature where mountains, mountain hiking or climbing is the focus? Whether it's mountain climbers in the Himalaya or mythical characters scaling mythical hills, the narrative and any pictures will portray the uphill portion but not the intervening descents that exist in almost all cases. Going back to the Bible, we read of ancient persons scaling the mountaintops but the impression, in biblical and most subsequent accounts, is that we climb/hike/scale up. Yes—but the little detail that "up" really entails up, down, up, down, up is glossed over or more accurately, outrightly omitted. We're conditioned to think "up" simply means up. Once on the trail, reality quickly takes over.

I'm not really complaining, nor did I on the day's hike —it was simply beautiful. We had seen Elk Ridge the day before, and as we drew nearer through the open meadows along Gullers Creek, then through forest until emerging from treeline, our spirits were buoyed. Again, I took numerous photos of flowers, including some from ground level with the

Northern Harrier hikes up Elk Ridge.

mountain in the distance. Later on, when we were asked the difficult-to-answer question, "What was your favorite part of the trail?" independent of each other, we each responded, "the Elk Ridge section."

In a similar vein, the flowers festooning the meadows on today's hike included a heretofore unseen species of which I, if compelled, would designate #1: the most beautiful of all that we saw. I'm referring to pinnate-leaved daisies whose golden yellowish orange centers were surrounded by petals of a light magenta. I can not envision any human-made construct, whether art or fashion or decor, in which this color combination would look "tasteful." But here on Elk Ridge in the Rocky Mountains this and any variety of hues was gorgeous without question. There's no such thing as the "wrong" color combination.

Rocci, Pocahontas, and Stahlberg caught us briefly but then we passed them while they stopped to cook a late breakfast. We didn't see them again until our evening campsite. During our brief conversation, Northern Harrier and I received the highest compliment imaginable, courtesy of Pocahontas: "Man, you guys kick butt." Music

Pinnate-leaved daisies were a favorite

to the ears of a couple of guys in their mid-60s when emanating from a young 20-something woman!

Predictably, the terrain became steeper as we approached Searle Pass where we saw our first marmot (the adorable furry rodent, not the windbreaker!). From this pass to the top of Elk Ridge, the elevation gain was no more than 300'. Intervening descents made our ascent more like 600-700', but take note that I didn't say "PUD," for the landscape was too breathtaking to imbibe in such negativity! Views were tremendous under predominantly sunny skies. Behind us, we looked back at the massive-looking Tenmile Range where we had just hiked two days ago. The backdrop ahead was some very high mountains (likely the Holy Cross Wilderness) beyond Tennessee Pass, where we'd hitch to Leadville tomorrow.

When we reached Kokomo Pass, identifiable with a sign (not common in the Rockies), we knew that we'd soon be descending the ridge. All through the alpine portion of the hike on both sides

66

of the two passes, streams & rivulets tumbled down the slope, birds flitted among the bushes (one I recognized was the white-crowned sparrow), and we saw more flowers than ever. The range of the latter's colors filled the entire spectrum. Rock cairns, a few of which resembled a miniature Tower of Babel, were placed strategically to ensure the trail's visibility. Scattered snowfields were large enough to beautify the setting without presenting an obstacle. With the breezes at the passes and the ridgeline making the air a bit too cold for stopping long, our lunch spot was in a sunny spot below treeline after Kokomo. In the bright sunshine, I managed to dry my tent, fly, groundcloth, and sleeping pad while we relaxed in the grass.

Immediately after lunch, the trail proceeded all downhill, which suited me fine as I became sluggish. The lack of a good night's sleep had caught up to me. The descent was very steep; we both remarked that we were grateful to hike in this direction as opposed to uphill. Near the bottom, we crossed Cataract Creek, named presumably for the little waterfall just before the bridge. With rain threatening (another typical Colorado Trail day with sun in early morning gradually giving way to rain clouds by afternoon), on went the pack covers and rain jackets. We hiked through an open area and neared Camp Hale, an old abandoned WWII training camp for cold weather, high altitude combat.

Since it was still early enough in the afternoon, we decided to start up the next slope where campsites and water supposedly awaited in less than a mile. Once again the guidebook failed us in that neither was present. Upon reaching a Forest Service road, we knew that we had gone too far per the guidebook which appeared to have mixed up the terms "north" and "south." Oh well, nothing's perfect. So we trudged on, hoping to reach Fiddler Creek which would put us only four-tenths of a mile short of U.S. Rt. 24, a major road crossing. Northern Harrier was completely out of water and my supply was minimal when we came to a flowing stream not mentioned in the book. Or, was it the stream mentioned as two-tenths of a mile "north" of the Forest Service road when, in fact, this one was south of it? This modest stream couldn't be Fiddler Creek which, per the guidebook, was spanned by a bridge. Even by western standards, it could hardly be considered a "creek." I suppose the sudden and unexpected appearance of this stream at a time when we both needed water (and at the end of the day to boot) was another form of Trail Magic.

Having reached a water source and uncertain at this point late in the day when we'd find water again, we decided then and there to make camp. Granted, the spot was not the best as it lay on sloped land with mosquitoes (well, I guess they're everywhere) and the noise of Rt. 24 traffic very palpable. But as usual on the trail, you make do. Arguably, this was our least desirable site but you know what? It didn't matter. In fact, most of the time on this hike, or any long-distance hike, you don't dwell on the detriments of where you sleep for the night. It's a bit like sticker shock syndrome or any situation where initial disappointment gives way to acceptance or even embracing what's before you; you make lemonade out of lemons. Maybe the campsite was far from perfect, but hiking 15.6 miles, ascending over 4,000' of elevation, and reveling in alpine splendor...priceless!

As we finished dinner, Rocci, Pocahontas, and Stahlberg happened by. Making the same assumption as we had, they were chagrined to find no water or campsites where the guidebook had identified such. Actually, their appearance was a gratifying confirmation that we hadn't misread the guidebook. After filling up with water, they moved on but we expected to run into them again tomorrow.

Since the next day was a low-mileage, nero day *cum* town stop (Leadville), we decided to sleep late—'til 5:30 am instead of 5:00! This short day with its minor elevation gain justified our extra time in the sack. The half-hour difference did bring more morning mosquitoes, but not as bothersome as last evening. If anything, their presence was a stimulus to keep moving.

After a steep uphill, we came upon the same threesome who were nearly out of matches. I had a book to spare so I lightened my load by giving it to them. I guess that was a small instance of Trail Magic. From our brief conversation, Rocci, Pocahontas, and Stahlberg told us that they were not planning a resupply stop in Leadville since their hike would end in a few days when they reached the Mt. Massive trailhead.

A stream flowed near their campsite, more substantial than the one where we camped. It didn't appear that this stream was mentioned in the guidebook. I guess such omission makes up for the absence of the stream that *was* mentioned. Was it Fiddler Creek? Then where was the bridge? As it turned out, we never found Fiddler Creek; we crossed no creeks with bridges as described in the book. This lapse became a standing joke for the next several days. Every time we crossed a stream regardless of the size, it was "Fiddler Creek" as in "that's Fiddler Creek," "I think we just crossed Fiddler Creek," "There's a bridge—this must be Fiddler Creek." On the whole, though, the guidebook had proved worth its weight and price. Mindful that we still had over 300 miles in front of us, I was treating it very tenderly when getting it out and placing it back in the pack.

Although last night's post-bedtime rain was brief, it was sufficient to coat our tents as well as all the grasses and bushes. Within a half-hour, my feet were soaked from the water penetrating through the socks. A few steep-but-brief uphills were all that kept the day from being super-easy. The nice part after crossing Rt. 24 and proceeding through a meadow and into the woods was when the Trail glommed onto an old railroad grade bed which we followed for the next two miles or so.

Arriving at the Tennessee Pass trailhead around 9:00, we started thumbing, but after ten minutes decided to phone the Leadville Hostel. While waiting, we said our final goodbyes to Rocci, Pocahontas, and Stahlberg as they rested before moving on. Like others we have met, they were quite fascinated with our attempt of a thru-hike. In response to Rocci's expressed interest in reading my on-line trail journal, I furnished him the website address.

While waiting, we also met a young northbound thru-hiker who shared the shuttle with us (as it turned out, against the rules because he did not intend to stay at the hostel). Rather taciturn to the point of being antisocial, he was evidently a "purist" who wanted to hike through Waterton Canyon despite the detour and mused about hiking it in the dark. He was unaware that the Colorado Trail's northernmost eight miles were closed.

The hostel owner "Wild Bill" picked us up and explained the policies and rules of the hostel during the ride down. Upon arrival, we were quite impressed with the setup as he showed us around. The hostel featured a large kitchen, lounge areas both on the main floor and downstairs, bunk rooms with lockers, showers, laundry, and free internet access available on the house computer. I took advantage of the computer to pay a bill (a vestige of "regular" off-trail life) as well as sift through scores of unread e-mail messages. A walk downtown to lunch was followed by my doing our laundry while Northern Harrier cycled to the Safeway to procure supplies for both of us. Another amenity offered by the hostel was the use of free bikes for local errands.

Situated at over 10,000' and surrounded by mountains, Leadville is the highest-elevation incorporated municipality in the U.S. and a virtual summertime mecca for outdoor enthusiasts of all stripes. To that end, our fellow hostel patrons included bikers (both mountain and road), day-hikers, and people just enjoying the high elevation climate. Although we met a few road cyclists, most of the bikers were of the mountain genre, training for the Leadville 100, a race scheduled to occur in two weeks. While the hostel appeared not to be full on this weeknight, there was still an abundance of guests. We talked to an ER doctor from Hawaii who was training for the upcoming bike event. Four women from Massachusetts had recently arrived to climb some 14ers—one had never been to Colorado. We engaged in interesting conversation with everyone, not only fellow guests but also Wild Bill's brother, Howard, who cooked all the meals when not sitting in the back yard smoking. It became apparent to me why Leadville Hostel was considered one of the best, at least from what I read on WhiteBlaze.net, an on-line chat room named after the AT but covering other trails quite extensively as well.

The hostel offered dinners and breakfasts with Howard presiding as the chief chef, so we signed up for both. Dinner featured chicken cordon bleu, potatoes, macaroni, salad, and beans—very tasty after a day on the trail. We served ourselves in the kitchen and then enjoyed our dinner around the dining room table, with some of us spilling onto the porch outside.

Still, we didn't meet any Colorado Trail or long-distance backpackers. It seemed like everyone was a mountain biker or an aspiring 14er (climbing the peaks over 14,000'). However, I did talk with a woman who was road biking. Hearing she hailed from El Paso, TX, I asked if she was acquainted with a cousin-once-removed of mine who lives there, and she recognized his name. She also told me that a woman named Mickey was also thru-hiking the Colorado Trail southbound and had stayed at the hostel last night; consequently, she was only one day ahead of us. Mickey was hiking solo although she was accompanied by a small dog. It was nice to at least be aware of a fellow southbounder whose hike somewhat coincided with ours, but both Northern Harrier and I doubted we'd catch up. However, you never know...

At the hostel, we did the usual chores of a town stop: wrote postcards, used the computer to check e-mail (again), peruse other websites, and update our trail journals. We also phoned the hostels that we'd reach later in the hike to provide an estimated arrival date and confirm that our maildrops were received. Thus far on this our fourth resupply stop, our packages had all been delivered intact without incident.

* * * * *

SO NOW THE HIKE WAS more than one-quarter complete and I felt pretty good, as did Northern Harrier. From the outset, he had maintained that Leadville was a watershed; successfully hiking the 143 miles to Leadville meant we had a good chance of persevering and finishing the entire Colorado Trail. I couldn't disagree, in fact, I knew where he was coming from.

There are two ways to approach a long-distance hike. They might seem paradoxical, but their relationship is not mutually exclusive. Focusing on the long haul, you're planning to hike the entire 482-mile trail. You want to hike it in a continuous trek. You have a clear goal that you hope to attain. However, if that's all you focus on, it can seem daunting, overwhelming in the early stages when you've hiked an impressive 140 miles, but still face over 300 challenging miles ahead.

So the other focus is one day at a time. Whether I was struggling in the modest hills of Segment 3 or marveling as I ascended and crossed the alpine wonderland of Georgia Pass and Elk Ridge, the extent to which I was looking ahead tended to be that night's campsite. In other words, I'm thinking "...another 3.5 miles," not "...417 miles to go." Although I never lost sight of those 417 miles, it wasn't a moment-by-moment hangup during the course of the day.

Northern Harrier thru-hiked the 2,184-mile AT so he's been there. He grasped the concept of the long-haul/short-term paradox. While less than one-quarter of the AT's length, the Colorado Trail was sufficiently long to engender the same approach. In contrast, Northern Harrier and I backpacked together on three trails in Pennsylvania of 70, 43, and 85 miles where the end of the trail/hike was as much on our mind—or more so—as daily progress.

Now it's not like **all** we think of is our daily progress and the end of each day's hike. We, of course, do look ahead at the long haul—and it still was a long haul! Accordingly, I saw two major upcoming challenges. One was the Collegiate Peaks after Twin

Lakes, where we would face our steepest ups and downs yet. A few days after the Collegiate Peaks, we would reach the Colorado Trail's halfway point a day short of U.S. Rt. 50 and access to Salida. Arriving in Salida would be an occasion to celebrate. Zero day perhaps?

The second challenge encompassed the 90-mile stretch between Salida and Creede. This remote location wasn't expected to be particularly difficult technically (famous last words!) but it featured long dry stretches where water scarcity would govern our schedule. And drawing on our experience to date, there loomed one more consideration not to lose sight of: some stretches which appear level on the elevation profile might, in fact, include PUDs. Thus far, there were virtually no "flat" parts of the Colorado Trail. But what would you expect? These are the Rocky Mountains!

Finally, I don't want to leave the impression that I'm hiking the Colorado Trail merely to "get somewhere," for this trek is as much about the journey as the destination. Or look at it this way: the "destination" is more than the night's campsite or the Durango trailhead. Alpine meadows, aspen groves, bristlecone forests, scenic vistas of mountains everywhere, fields of flowers at all elevations—aren't all of these phenomena the "true" destinations?

Rocks of the Rockies — Tennessee Pass to Clear Creek Road

"We joked that we were hiking Colorado at times and New Hampshire at times..."
Day 13 — August 5, 2011

L EADVILLE WAS A TREAT—BOTH THE TOWN and the hostel—but our one "nero" day was sufficient, so it was time to move on. A scrumptious hostel breakfast of eggs, potatoes, pancakes and fruit began at 7:30 am. "Wild Bill" deposited us at the trailhead just before 9:00. We thanked him for running such a wonderful hostel and serving so many people.

Today's hike was easy for the first four miles, enabling us to set a vigorous pace. Then the ups and downs started over very rocky terrain that was reminiscent of New England. We joked that we were hiking Colorado at times and New Hampshire at times, the latter when deep in the forest. Our three ascents today were statistically not much. None exceeded 500' of elevation but I found the first one particularly difficult. For the next two, I took Northern Harrier's advice and successfully changed my walking pattern to take shorter steps and it helped. Northern Harrier was still ahead of me; he was quite strong on the ascents. The rockiness caused me to proceed more deliberately on the descents.

Entering the Holy Cross Wilderness, I thought back to my failed hike there in 1998 when elevation sickness did me in. I also realized firsthand how decent aerobic fitness does not necessarily translate into easy acclimation. At that time, I jogged four miles

The rock-strewn trail reminded us of New Hampshire's White Mountains.

per day and had even jogged on the mile-high streets of Denver during the business trip preceding the hike. But I still experienced nausea and vomiting on my second day as I ascended. At least on this hike, all that concern was behind me, knock on wood.

Today wasn't all rocks and deep forest. The mountains glistened with patches of snow; we even walked through a little. The above-treeline sections, while brief, gave us both distant views and more wildflower sightings.

The peculiar phenomenon today was that where there was water, camping was nigh impossible because of the rocky terrain. And some nice campsites were located nowhere near water. We had decided to hike beyond the last good (so designated by the guidebook) campsite with water near Bear Lake and continue up yet another steep ascent. The hours passed on but no water with suitable campsites was found as we reached the end of Segment 9. The guidebook told us that we need only walk four-tenths of a mile to Glacier Creek for water with "good campsites," and since we didn't want to camp at the segment trailhead, on we went. The clear, briskly-flowing waters of Glacier Creek belied the name (normally, creeks and streams emanating from glaciers are an opaque slate gray) but alas, we didn't see any "good campsites" in the vicinity. Chagrined, we inched further along the trail while scanning the woods carefully until Northern Harrier found an opening in the trees a hundred feet or so off the trail with a fire ring about one-tenth of a mile beyond the creek. Gratefully we settled in, watched a trio of birds peck at my food waste, and retired around 7:45 pm which was past our "hiker midnight." Considering that this morning's start was roughly three hours later than "normal" (because of our staying in the hostel), our hiking 14 miles for the day was quite satisfying.

As it turned out, the camping scene at Glacier Creek portended the remainder of the trail until Salida (U.S. Rt. 50). Most of the good water sources, e.g. creeks similar to Glacier Creek, ran where two ridges merged; consequently, the adjacent terrain was steep and wooded with no ideal places to pitch tents. I didn't mind a little slope as long as I didn't roll out of the tent opening! Now at this point, my hiker friends who use hammocks in lieu of tents would say "You should..." And my response would be, to quote the late folksinger Allen Wayne Dameron's line, "Don't 'should' on me, and I won't 'should' on you!"

We were also buoyed by today's perfect weather—the first day of the hike where we had zero rain. That is, until 11:30 pm, when thunder and lightning ensued. The small amount of actual rain that the sky unleashed proved just enough to wet the outside of the tents and the ground, meaning we again packed wet gear in the morning. Taking for granted that we're the early birds—surely no one else is around at 5:30 am—we were surprised when a trio of young women came running by. This reminded us that today was Saturday and we'd likely see an abundance of fellow trail users, especially considering that the segment would end at the trailhead parking lot for Mt. Elbert, Colorado's highest peak, rising to 14,433'.

Today featured two 1,000' ascents plus a 500' ascent to begin Segment 11. After an easy mile to start, we slogged up a saddle of Sugarloaf Mountain. Being early in the day, I felt fresh as usual and handled the ascent well. After a ridge walk and descent, the next 1,000' ascent to an unnamed ridge gave us views of Leadville. On the ascent, we met another southbound Colorado Trail thru-hiker. Chris appeared to be in his early 30s and sported a very heavy pack. A pleasant conversation revealed that he had hiked much of the AT in the South and his pack's weight was augmented by a barrel-shaped canister in which to store his food. "It's not the bears I'm worrying about, but the little critters such as mice, chipmunks, etc. They got into my pack in North Carolina." Although he started about a week before us, an ankle injury sustained at Searle Pass had slowed him. He caught up to us while we were having lunch just down from the ridge. After that, we passed him again and didn't see him any more. With our apparently faster pace, I didn't expect to see him again, but you never know. Talking to Chris reminded me that we had not yet run into Eric, the thru-hiker we had met over Tenmile Range a few days ago.

We were hiking Segment 10, which looks very similar to Segment 9 on paper: same exact distance, same elevation change. But today's footing was much more forgiving—predominantly a dirt path with less rocks on the trail, even in those parts where the woods surrounding the corridor were rocky. Although views were limited, the verdant evergreens were pretty and healthy looking. Catching occasional views of 14,421' Mt. Massive, we couldn't be certain if we also saw Mt. Elbert. Given that the two giants' elevations differ by a mere twelve feet, I wondered how could one differentiate between them when hiking up or viewing from the base level. Just follow the signs, right?

We engaged in conversation with a runner on top of the second climb. He was a pacer for the upcoming Leadville 100, a mountain race of 100 miles. His wife was a Forest Service ranger. We never met any other Forest Service staff on the hike.

The closer we got to the Massive/Elbert trailhead marking the end of Segment 10, the more people we encountered. A few were curious enough to ask about our hike. All were impressed at our attempt to reach Durango. At the trailhead parking lot, a woman offered us water. Little acts of kindness like this are very much appreciated.

Since we were making good time, we decided to continue 3.3 more miles to Herrington Creek, but only after enjoying a foot soak in the creek at the trailhead. Moving on, we ascended 500' gradually while meeting scores of day-hikers returning from Mt. Elbert, presumably having "bagged" another 14er—not just any 14er, but Colorado's highest peak. Once we passed the side trail leading up to Elbert, we met no one else. Pulling into our campsite around 4:00 pm capped a record-breaking 16-mile day. An exquisite campsite under soft-needled pine trees in an open area was quite pleasant, except like nearly every night's abode, the mosquitoes were vicious.

I felt pretty good at this point, as did Northern Harrier, but we still harbored apprehension about the steep climbs awaiting us in Segments 12 and 13. They'd been on our minds for several days. Day after tomorrow, we'd find out firsthand just how arduous they were.

As was the case last night, no rains came as we prepared dinner. From those with whom we conversed in Leadville and other places who were more familiar with the Rockies, we heard that the "monsoon" season usually ended by mid-July. This tidbit was nice to know but we weren't counting on zero rain herein.

About 6:45, just as I was ready for shuteye, a hiker came along. Contrary to my prediction, it was Chris. He told us he was basically a late up/late start/late finish type of hiker. Today, he had spent even more time than usual talking to all the day-hikers. Tonight marked the first occasion in which we shared a campsite with a fellow hiker so we talked past "hiker midnight." Chris considered us "experts" in light of our experience of hiking the entire AT and other trails. While demurring from the sobriquet, Northern Harrier couldn't resist dispensing some advice on how to lighten his pack. We explained that we were early-to-bed, early-to-rise types and promised to be quiet in the morning.

78

* * * * *

So ON SUNDAY MORNING, August 7, 2011, two weeks now into the hike, we finally awoke having experienced a totally dry night. That's right: no rain at any time! Even the inside of the tent fly was dry this morning. And cold! The stars were magnificent and still quite prominent when I emerged from the tent to begin the morning rituals. Brrr! It felt to me like the coldest morning of the hike thus far until Northern Harrier reminded me of the frost that we endured in the Lost Creek Meadow way back on Day 4. Quite true. Remembering my frozen hands, I agreed that the discomfort of that morning was worse. The drier atmosphere here was friendlier to the body.

And the dawn scene was friendly to the eyesight. In particular, the morning sunlight glowing on the aspen trees was enchanting. No two trees assumed the same coloration or brightness. It all depended on what tree and what part of each tree the sun's rays struck. Aspens exemplify the uniqueness of the western deciduous forest. A quick superficial glance reminds one of birches in a Northern New England hardwood zone. However, a closer look reveals that aspens' bark doesn't peel, the leaves are different, and at times, the famously reputed "quaking" readily confirms their identity. Aspens are just one more enjoyable feature of this magnificent trail.

Only 4.4 miles to Rt. 82 and a one-mile road walk would take us to the Twin Lakes general store and post office, our fifth mail-

Aspen groves were one enchanting feature of the Colorado Trail.

79

drop stop and largest to-date as our boxes contained the 5-6 days of food that we needed for the hike to Salida. Chris never stirred as we packed up and started the uphill trek where we'd catch views of the lakes before descending. Up, then down: typical of the Colorado Trail. The morning chill stayed with us; for the first time on this hike, I wore gloves in the early going.

We passed some early morning would-be climbers of Mt. Elbert coming our way. Before long, we happened by viewpoints where the two large lakes lay ahead, the morning sun sparkling on the blue waters. I admit that they looked picturesque. Earlier I had expressed to Northern Harrier my disdain for "phony" lakes, to which he was indifferent:

"They're man-made because they're reservoirs. No big deal. They're needed for water supply. They still look nice."

"Now you're a big fan of Maine and New Hampshire. They have real lakes up there."

"They also have reservoirs, like on the Kennebec River."

"Well, yeah I know. So's Flagstaff Lake below Saddleback. But they're not as nice as the real lakes."

"So are Twin Lakes real or not?"

Actually that question did not lend itself to a yes/no answer. From what I gathered in reading the guidebook, the lakes were natural lakes where a resort initially flourished in the 19th century, but subsequently were expanded and made into reservoirs.

The lakes loomed larger during the descent to Rt. 82, which seemed to take longer than expected. The trail wound through a dry forest followed by open areas increasingly resembling desert more than the Rocky Mountains as we continued our downhill pace, losing 1,200' of elevation. Reaching the highway at 8:20 am, we walked one mile to Twin Lakes village where the store was closed until 9:00. A nice guy with a key let us in to pick up our supply boxes from the post office portion of the still-dark store. We set to work reassembling all of our food bags, having to find capacity in our backpacks for more meals than we'd hauled thus far.

Things were still quiet on this Sunday morning. A few cabins were visible but not many people stirred yet. Almost ready to resume the hike, we resigned ourselves to a slight uphill road walk back to the trail intersection when Trail Magic intervened.

I had finished re-packing before Northern Harrier and was looking for a trash can when a car pulled up. A middle-aged man emerged and started walking to the store.

Me: "It's still closed—we heard they're opening late today, probably 9:30."

Him: "Oh, OK. I was just looking to buy some souvenirs before we leave. We'll find some somewhere else."

"We were able to get inside, but only for our packages in the post office portion. The store itself was still closed. We had sent packages to ourselves with supplies. We're backpacking the Colorado Trail."

"Wow, that's amazing! We're on vacation and doing a little hiking but not overnight. Where did you start?"

"Near Denver two weeks ago today. We're hiking to Durango. If all goes well as planned, we're hiking 480 miles."

"That's something—I'm really impressed!"

"Are you driving east [pointing to the way we came] by any chance? We walked a mile down this highway from where the trail intersects it and would appreciate a lift back."

"It would be an honor to take you. We can throw your packs on top of the car and make room inside for you."

"Thanks so much. I see the store's open now. My friend is almost ready but can you wait just a minute while we buy something inside?"

"Sure! I'll get the car ready and I'd better tell my wife."

With that, he swung the car around the parking area and alongside our now-full packs and hoisted himself up on top where three bicycles were strapped into roof racks. I didn't see how he'd squeeze our packs up there but somehow he did. I also didn't see how we'd fit into the car whose occupants included his wife and three young daughters. Our benefactor's name was Bart. The family hailed from Northern California and had spent time in Yosemite before coming to Colorado for the rest of their vacation. They were starting the homeward stretch today.

We continued chatting on the short ride back up the road during which one daughter sat on her mother's lap while the other two squeezed between Northern Harrier and me in the back seat. Manifestly illegal, I'm sure! They were all very interested in our hike, firing off questions (what did we eat, how did we sleep, did we see any bears, how many miles did we hike each day, etc.) and bidding us good luck as they dropped us off. What a nice family! What a stroke of luck! How unexpected! My approaching Bart and starting a conversation which led to expressing our need for a ride (a practice known to long-distance hikers as "yogiing") didn't change the fact that we had received true Trail Magic!

Finding ourselves back on the trail before 10:00, we marveled at our good fortune. For the next five miles, the trail circled the lake approaching a dam at the far end with gentle but persistent rolling ups and downs. Rapidly-increasing temperatures in a full sun made conditions tantamount to desert walking. Northern Harrier set the pace as usual but didn't stride as fast as he normally would on a stretch like this. For this, I was grateful and told him so. An unspoken consensus had called for us pacing ourselves with newly-stuffed (read: heavy) packs hiking in the hot open sun. At least it was still relatively early in the day.

Just past the dam, we talked with four mountain bikers (took a group photo for them) and again answered questions about our hike. They offered water, insisting that they could spare their supply because their biking for the day was almost done. I accepted a small amount while jokingly expressing misgivings about increasing my pack weight! Like many others we met, they expressed their admiration for our thru-hiking. We never let these compliments go to our heads, for much of the trail lay ahead of us. But without question, our morale, not to say egos, were boosted.

Lunch was had in the shade on the lake's south side. "Shade" in this area is elusive unless you come to a cluster of ponderosa pines. Even here, it was still fleeting. I moved my position several times as the sun's rays found their way past the sparse foliage of the evergreens.

Turning from the lake, the CDT splits from the Colorado Trail. After 99 miles together, the CDT's veering off took it straight toward Hope Pass. I never looked up the official place-name origin but in the guidebook's segment tip authored by Gudy Gaskill, Hope Pass was described as "...you *hope* you'll never have to hike over it again!" Until recently, the Colorado Trail also traversed the pass until a re-route changed its path. Subsequent to our hike, this upcoming portion of the CDT has been designated (actually, re-designated) as a portion of the Colorado Trail, forming an 80-mile loop from Twin Lakes where we now stood until the trails joined again south of Salida on the Monarch Crest. In effect, a Colorado Trail thru-hiker now faces a choice to hike either route.

For our hike, the only choice was the left turn where we began a steep, steady ascent on what proved to be the most exerting part of the day. We encountered a few more bikers and day-hikers. Our goal was a stream beyond the segment's Mile 15, but the very faint "flow" of the first two streams that we crossed caused some concern about water availability in this stretch. At least our early start and fast exit from Twin Lakes enabled us to keep going. And fortunately, the water gods were with us as we found a more substantial creek with a level-enough place to camp at Segment Mile 16.7. Another day was complete.

Guess what? We had mosquitoes. Again! And how have I dealt with them since I seem to mention them every day? Northern Harrier used an insect repellant that also doubled as a sunscreen—a pretty handy way to multitask. Eschewing chemical remedies, I've promptly changed into long pants and long-sleeve shirt upon reaching camp. When the bugs are particularly obnoxious, I've also put on the windbreaker with the hood over my head. Some evenings I resorted to eating while walking around rather than sitting, which normally violates a backpacker's principle: don't stand when you can sit, don't sit when you can lie (down, that is). There are exceptions, but many hikers avoid any extra effort since it's enough of an exertion to hike 12, 15, 18 miles on the trail with our full packs. Side trips (e.g. the mere one mile to the Twin Lakes store) are kept to a minimum as we strive to prevent the extra strain on our knees, feet and the rest of our body. That's why we prefer to hitch rides instead. This concept holds when reaching the campsite: Conserve yourself. Fill your water in one trip to the creek. Only hike up that tempting-looking knoll if you're sure that a nice view awaits. Hang your food bag from a tree far enough away, but not too far. Don't walk too much.

Unless it's the best way to escape the bugs.

With 182 miles in the books, we now looked at less than 300 miles remaining, which still seemed like a lot. Before tomorrow's end, this hike would become my personal second-longest. I'd found that as long as I got a good night's sleep (for me at least nine hours), I was pretty strong and could hike 15 miles. But when we entered the Collegiate Peaks tomorrow, we'd see just how strong we really were.

In our tents by 6:45 pm, I started to drift off when I heard voices. Peering from my tent, I observed two backpackers hiking from the same direction as us. I was sure that they'd try to set up camp near us as they glanced at our tents, but they moved on. Maybe we'd meet them tomorrow? But as it turned out, we didn't see any sign of them when we arose at 5:15 am after another rainless, cloudless, and cold night. This was the first morning in which I wore my fleece sweater, gloves, and hat in the campsite. Off by 6:25 with the gloves still on, I didn't feel that I had a quality night's sleep (quantity-wise, 10 hours seems more than adequate!). Consequently, I didn't feel as vigorous as most mornings.

84

Fortunately the first few miles were easy until finishing our descent into a broad valley (probably part of the privately-owned Clear Creek Ranch) where we then faced a 500' ascent. Steep in most places, the climb warmed us up and wore us out (a little). PEE came into play; we were looking ahead to the steep ascent after Clear Creek into the Collegiate Peaks and didn't expect this intervening knob. It's similar to when the #10 ranked NCAA basketball team looks ahead to next week's game against #1 and overlooks tomorrow's game against a tough but unranked opponent.

Despite still being early in the day, the long descent into Clear Creek Valley was hot in a landscape devoid of trees; in this respect, it was similar to the walk around Twin Lakes. We had descended to 8,937', the first time we found ourselves below 9,000' since Segment 4 at the beginning of Lost Creek Wilderness nearly150 miles ago. Being the end of a segment (#11), the Clear Creek Valley featured a road and drive-in campsites with a fair amount of campers. One of the RVs' denizens talked to us for the entire time as we rested by the creek and filled our water bottles. With my mind on the steep climb ahead of us, I didn't remember a thing he said.

Steep and Steeper — Clear Creek Road to Salida

"What's that expression—start slow and then slow down? That was our approach on this ascent."
Day 17 — August 9, 2011

D ON'T TAKE MY word for it:

"Without a doubt, this is the defining characteristic of this segment: A steep up and down followed by another steep up and down."

"The descent to the Avalanche Trailhead is very steep—one trail user noted he wouldn't have minded a belay in a few places! Trekking poles come in handy here."

To put in perspective the above statements from the guidebook's introductions to Segments 12 and 13 respectively, the word "steep" rarely occurs throughout the remainder of the book. Only in the stretch we were starting now was the word "steep" used to describe the segment as a whole. Statistically, Segment 12's ratio of feet of elevation gained to miles hiked was the second highest of all 28 segments, exceeded only by Segment 7's traverse of Tenmile Range. Our packs were lighter on that portion because of our slackpack. The only reason Segment 13's comparable statistics rank lower is that the segment's 23-mile length brings down the average; most of the elevation change occurs in the first six miles.

At least we knew what awaited us—no PEE here. So on Monday, August 8, our 16th day on the trail, we began the ascent at 9:20 am. I've already said that I liked straight uphills *sans* PUDs, especially for the rewards inherent at the summit. The first part of that statement rang true, but not the second; we were ascending 2,900' in 4.3 miles to a forested ridge of Waverly Mountain where we likely would see little in the way of views.

To my mild surprise, we met two parties of three hikers each, all men, backpacking in the same direction. The first group was just out for two nights. The other hikers were faster/stronger and were section hiking to Salida. I thought that this point, being further from Denver on a weekday meant we'd have the trail to ourselves; shows what I knew. But I didn't mind; it's not like the trail was overcrowded, and they were all pleasant guys.

The ascent was quite laborious. We made it to the undistinguished ridgetop by 1:00 pm, stopping partway up for lunch. Even though the slope was forested, the thin and narrow foliage of Western trees permitted plenty of penetration from the sun's rays. I couldn't believe how hot it felt at an elevation exceeding 11,600'! As expected, no vistas presented themselves—not much in the way of a payoff for our slog except for the satisfaction that we had conquered our first summit in the Collegiate Peaks range. But the high point did bless us with one thrilling reward: the trees at this level included bristlecone pines, the sight of which made for quite an awesome thought when you realize that these trees have been around a few thousand years.

This dearth of sweeping, or any, views as a reward for our 3,000' slog reminded me of typecasting regarding eastern vs. western hiking. More than once, I've heard westerners assert that their disdain for eastern hiking is all those trees! The trees obscure views in such a way that the East doesn't feature the expansive, wide-open vistas of the West. In one particular such dialog with a former colleague who lived in Las Vegas, I suggested that he hike the White Mountains of New Hampshire, whose views might remind him at least a tad bit of the West. I'm not sure he believed me. In any case, this first ascent of the Collegiate Peaks belies the whole stereotype of the West's breathtaking vistas; here we were at 11,600' in a picturesque and lovely forest to be sure, but devoid of views. Not a complaint, just an observation...

We didn't linger long at ridgeline but set forth down the other side to Pine Creek on a hot sunny descent of 1,200' in 1.6 miles. This pretty body of water was the first of two "Pine Creeks" on the Colorado Trail—can't they come up with more imaginative names? We met the first party of three resting at the creek. They were planning to camp and fish at Rainbow Lake tonight, as was the other threesome. Responding to Northern Harrier's inquiry, they told us that the lake was accessed via a three-tenths of a mile side trail after hiking 1.7 miles up another 1,000' of elevation.

Camping on a lake sounded nice, something we hadn't done yet. Should we continue on? We considered doing so as it was still early, but decided to stay put for the night. We were both pretty tired. Look at it this way: we hiked 11.2 miles. Granted, this was a low mileage day for us, but we hiked up some very steep ascents and the descent to Pine Creek wasn't exactly a stroll in the park. Continuing on to Rainbow Lake only gained us 1.6 more miles and would render us more fatigued than we felt now. Moreover, Pine Creek was a more-than-suitable camping locale. Camping here put us in good stead for tomorrow's straight-up ascent first thing in the morning when we're strong. Decision made: up went the tents on a small knoll, but occasional strong winds chased Northern Harrier to a site further up the trail where a denser tree cover lessened the wind's effect on his lightweight tent.

After three days of essentially cloudless weather, large puffy clouds passed over head occasionally blocking the sun. I washed myself partially in the clear, pristine-looking Pine Creek but the winds and water were too cold for a complete bath. As such, they presented quite a contrast to the hot sun. But brisk winds and cold water didn't deter Northern Harrier; as he's frequently done in the creeks we've camped by, he again administered a full body wash, emerging none the worse for it. In the context of a hike, "full body wash" pointedly excludes soap, detergent, lotions, oils, etc. Soap may be cleansing to our bodies, but its effect on the natural environment is quite the opposite. Pure cold water from the mountain streams still removes a fair amount of dirt, sweat, and grime.

We bade goodby to the other hikers as they moved on. Later, a father-son tandem out to find a base camp and scale 14ers stopped by briefly before continuing on. They were followed by two horseback riders. Like nearly every night to date, we had no campsite companions.

As of today, this hike had become my second-longest. Only my 2005 Northern New Hampshire-to-Mt. Katahdin AT hike, a 300-miler, was longer than the 194 miles we'd hiked since Indian Creek, which seemed like an eternity ago. Hopefully that record would tumble in less than two weeks.

Looking ahead to tomorrow, we figured on 12 miles to finish Segment 12, starting with a 1,400' ascent right-off-the-bat. Then it would be on to Segment 13, still in the Collegiate Peaks, with another monster ascent/descent. At that point, a town stop might be greatly appreciated. Perhaps an unscheduled R&R stop at Buena Vista would be in order? Under these circumstances, you don't want to rule anything out.

At times, I had regretted bringing my warmer-but-heavier sleeping bag, but not now on another clear, cloudless and cold night. It had been several days without rain for which I was grateful. If given a choice between cold and dry vs. warm and rainy, I'll take the cold any time! Although our tents were out of sight from each other, Northern Harrier and I both arose at the normal 5:00 am and were ready to leave by 6:10. Shedding the fleece sweater and hat, I led the way up the 1,400' ascent of the Mt. Harvard massif. If one didn't know the name of the range over which we were now trekking, the names Harvard, Columbia, Yale, and Princeton provided a hint. No, it's not the Ivy League! There's also Mt. Oxford. The names were dubbed by early geologists and explorers who chose to honor their alma maters. Thus the sobriquet "Collegiate Peaks" was born. Sounds like some cerebral geologists! One such gentleman was Josiah Whitney, for whom the continental U.S.'s highest peak in California is named. Mr. Whitney may have been cerebral but he wasn't too open-minded when he rejected John Muir's theory of the glaciers' role in creating the Sierra. Dismissing Muir as a mere "sheepherder," Whitney was subsequently proved wrong. But that's another story.

Unlike yesterday afternoon's climb which was largely devoid of rewards, this one took us through some alpine areas on the last quarter-mile to the summit, making the trek more scenic. Typical of early morning, the sun was pleasantly warm while the shade was cool. Like yesterday, we enjoyed walking through a forest of bristlecone pines at the summit.

Early morning shadows in the Collegiate Peaks.

Most of the rest of the morning was gradual descent with a few intervening ascents. One highlight was seeing a grouse, probably a blue grouse, strutting across the trail and putting on a show for us by puffing his throat. Actually, the show was more likely intended for a female but we still enjoyed it. We gradually descended from a moist forest with frequent streams to a dry forest consisting of thickly growing small Ponderosa pines.

While some of the trail was dirt or pine needles, much of it was filled with loose rocks. My left foot became sore from stepping on all the rocks, forcing me to begin treading with more deliberation. At our lunch spot on Three Elk Creek, a foot soak eased things somewhat, but the frigid water kept me from too long a bathing.

We approached Harvard Lakes, two small bodies of water set in a dense forest. Here, we met some day-hikers, our first fellow forest travelers of the day. The final steep descent into the canyon/valley of Cottonwood Creek/North Fork was open, desert-like terrain again, somewhat taxing because the sun was now high and hot. On the other hand, I appreciated how these surroundings provided another example of the Colorado Trail's diversity.

All good descents (and all less-than-good descents) come to an end. We found ourselves at the bottom before 1:00 pm and unlike yesterday at Pine Creek, this time we would move on. But not before we passed up some Trail Magic. A man we had met and talked with briefly at Harvard Lakes pulled up in his car at the trailhead just before we resumed our hike and asked if we wanted a ride to Buena Vista. Although somewhat tempted (Town food! Bed! Showers!), we declined the nice offer. It's funny: 24 hours ago, we would have jumped at the chance, but now we were looking forward to continuing our pace and camping at Silver Creek Lakes on a brief, relatively-level stretch partway up the Mt. Yale massif. Still, it was a nice gesture for which we thanked him.

Psyching ourselves up for tackling this next slope, we met a young woman with her two dogs out day-hiking. She planned an ascent of Mt. Yale. "Hmmm—it seemed awfully late in the day to begin a 14er," I thought to myself. From our conversation, she had hiked most of the AT in 2005, the same year that I hiked over 700 miles to finish it. She also hiked much of the Colorado Trail this year until an injury forced her off the trail. Bluebird (real name Terri) was from Georgia and drove a camper van. We talked for a while, then she started up. After giving Bluebird a ten-minute head start, we began the hot and steep ascent.

91

What's that expression—start slow and then slow down? That was our approach on this ascent. I don't know how best to portray the elevation profile: an arrowhead? A Hershey's Kiss? An idealized Christmas tree? But at least we knew that more-than-adequate time remained for us to reach Silver Creek Lakes. On the ascent, I reverted to inhaling through my nose again because my throat was dry and raspy. Early in the hike, Northern Harrier urged me to breathe through my mouth, which meant that two middle-aged marathon runners from Southeastern Pennsylvania prescribed conflicting advice on how to breathe while hiking uphill. My hiking partner on the 2006 John Muir Trail hike recommended long inhales through the nose and short exhales via the mouth, a technique that worked well at the time.

We took several short breaks, including one when we caught up to Bluebird. At that point, she wisely decided to turn back and retry first thing in the morning. I was relieved for her because 3:00 pm was much too late to climb another 3,500' to Mt. Yale's summit.

Wishing Bluebird well, we trudged on and reached Silver Creek Lakes before 4:00. Success! Feeling pretty good that we made it to this point, we were now poised for the final 900' ascent first thing tomorrow when we'd feel fresh. Fortuitously, Mt. Yale's steep incline levels off for about a half-mile which proved sufficient to find suitable places to pitch our tents. Our site was ideal as the nearby stream, pine-needled ground under trees giving us the feel of a cushy carpet, an open meadow, two small lakes, and the Collegiate Peaks lording over us all combined to enhance our satisfaction at having made substantial progress in these two segments.

We had been in camp for about an hour when three hikers we had met yesterday came by: Marty, his son Patrick, and Patrick's friend Adam. They had camped last night at Rainbow Lake. We talked with them for a long time before they moved ahead. They were obviously very strong hikers.

Also present at the campsite was the roofless remains of an old cabin. I cooked inside its walls to partially escape the increasingly-blowing winds which played havoc with my stove's flame. By 6:00, the winds had abated and it was quite cool in the shade, although not enough to deter the mosquitoes. Would we ever leave them behind us?

Expecting that the 11,000'+ elevation here—our highest camp to-date—would make this our coldest night, I took one last gaze at Mt. Yale, before succumbing to hiker midnight. But not before reflecting with gratitude that I was pretty sure I had lost weight. I would certainly hope so after over 200 miles! I wondered what the scale would show.

$$* * * * *$$

AT THIS ELEVATION, WE EXPECTED a cold morning. Deciding to sleep until 5:30 am, we were surprised that the morning was the warmest in a while. I didn't even wear the fleece sweater outside the tent.

For whatever reason, I didn't sleep very well. Northern Harrier even remarked how I seemed restless (and he wears ear plugs!). Nonetheless, I led the ascent up the flank of Mt. Yale, an ascent that was very steep like yesterday afternoon, but at least shorter. Once on the ridgeline, the trail turned left before reaching the high point where we met a couple who had camped there last night after climbing the Yale summit. Another 14er down for them.

A few views were had, but the descent into the tree cover started almost as soon as we reached the ridge. Again, there were bristlecone pines near the top. Before long though, we left the forest as a steep, rocky descent took us, like the previous few days, through open, dry country devoid of trees and resembling an arid, semi-desert ecosystem. Although it was still early (9:30), the hot sun had already made its presence known when we reached Avalanche Trailhead, where we faced another 2.3 mile descent to

South Cottonwood Creek. This latter portion reminded me of some Maine AT descents in that some PUDs made it seem like more up-hill than downhill!

I wasn't happy with the Colorado Trail this morning. It seemed that we were walking on steep and rough (though well-marked) trail with little reward other than occasional views of some 14ers and the broad valley to the East. Along that valley lay the towns of Buena Vista and further on, Salida. Much of this area was dry mountain forest with fewer flowers than we saw on our first ten days. Drawing on my John Muir Trail experience of hiking at similar elevations, I had also expected alpine lakes in the high country that we had just put behind us, and yet we only passed by a few small ponds in the forest. Actually, there was no logic behind my expectations. I should have realized by now that the Colorado Trail was more different from the JMT than similar.

Anyway, lunch at the South Cottonwood Creek was followed by an 800' ascent through a dry forest to a saddle. Here, I tried the cell phone to make reservations for the Simple Hostel in Salida where we had sent ourselves supply boxes. Unfortunately, we were scheduled to arrive on a Friday and they were booked! Bummer! We had not made reservations earlier because of uncertainty as to which exact day we'd reach Salida.

We discussed options. Northern Harrier called his wife, Charlene, and obtained a list of motels. We called a Days Inn: $129! For a Days Inn! We reserved a room for Saturday night and decided to camp at the trailhead by U.S. Route 50 on Friday. This was not what we wanted!

Although this development put us in a funk, we responded with a vigorous and steady pace from the ridgetop to Dry Creek. In less than two hours over rolling terrain, slabbing a mountain pock-marked with ridges and slopes, we hiked without pausing until reaching the creek, 4.3 miles later. It was ironic that this part's first two creeks mentioned in the guidebook—Silver Prince and Maxwell—barely evinced any water whereas the discouragingly-named Dry Creek was flowing nicely. Typical of our other camping locales near creeks running between the converging slopes, we managed to create spaces for our tents up the incline from the creek on semi-level ground in a grove of mixed evergreens and aspens.

Northern Harrier forges ahead.

Still mulling about our Salida options, we noticed that our cell phones indicated that service was available so we called the hostel again. They had a cancellation! We were in, at least for Friday, as Saturday was still booked. John, the owner, said he'd find something for us Saturday so that we could enjoy our first zero day of the hike. So we ended the day upbeat. Now it was just a matter of another 27 miles until attaining the simple pleasures of a bed and shower. And in those two days, we would pass the Colorado Trail's halfway point.

As we were finishing dinner, two guys came by and introduced themselves as Mike and Austin. They were father and son. As it turned out, we had been crisscrossing and leapfrogging each other for a while. They were the two hikers I saw from my tent three nights ago. They usually started and finished later in the day than us, so they often hiked past our campsites after our "hiker midnight" when we had retired for the evening. Mike and Austin recognized our tents: "So you have the Mountain Hardwear tent." It wasn't clear to me how we passed them in the mornings without seeing them; I surmised that they camped out-of-sight.

Shortly afterward, a woman accompanied by a small dog appeared. "Mickey," I thought, remembering the description given to me from the biker in Leadville. Yes, this slender, short-haired woman was Mickey. We had caught up to her because like us, she had an offer (from the same guy) for the free shuttle to Buena Vista and, unlike us, she took advantage of it.

All of a sudden, feeling hospitable perhaps because we finally had met some *bona fide* thru-hikers (*"bona fide"* meaning they had made it this far like us), I rose to my feet and thrust a grubby hand into my food bag:

"Here Austin, would you like a piece of dried ginger?"

Hesitation. "Uh, I don't know. Don't think I've ever tried it."

"It tastes good—at least I think so. He [Northern Harrier] doesn't care for it, but try a small piece. Ginger is a natural anti-inflammatory." He tried it.

"Mickey, do you want a piece?" She had the appearance of someone who was open to healthy and/or natural foods.

"Uh, I've never had it before. Is it strong?"

"Yeah, a little, but it's not bad in small bites. You can see there's sugar on top." She also tried a piece.

All three of them were southbound thru-hikers. Mike and Austin were to be met by family in Salida while Mickey was going to the Simple Lodge and Hostel and, like us, spending two nights and taking a zero day. She already had her reservations.

Mike and Austin were inclined to hike further this evening until I pointed out that there were no more water sources before a long road walk coming up; this was why we had ended here at Dry Creek after only 13.7 miles. The three of them tented near us on the other side of the creek.

* * * * *

HAVING LESS DAYLIGHT over the nearly three weeks since beginning this hike, our 5:00 am wake-ups were forcing us to do more of our morning chores in darkness. I remarked how bright the stars still seemed this morning. But it was definitely worth it, especially in the first hour (the "Golden Hour") when we watched the sun rise, appreciating the alpenglow on the next and final "Ivy Leaguer," Mt. Princeton. Like nearly all of our campsites near creeks, we started uphill with a very steep quarter-mile or so. In the initial climb, the perfect early morning photo-op presented itself. Northern Harrier was about 50' ahead of me and about to turn near the ridgecrest when I yelled, "Stop!" His silhouette against the sky was perfect; the full outline of his backpack-toting figure stood in shadow against the pre-sunrise dawn sky. This was the kind of photo-op that would only last a minute or two. We were at the right place at the right time. In the subsequent 40 seconds in which we traded places for him to photograph me in the same position, the sky had already changed. Five minutes later, the crimson slope of Mt. Princeton cried out for what I was convinced would be a prize-winning photo.

A mere 1.2 fast miles found us at a Forest Service road and the beginning of a 5.7 mile road walk. This longest such walk on the Colorado Trail was necessitated because the "natural" trail corridor lay on a large tract of private land closed to the public. Such hard, flat surfaces are normally dismal but our early start mitigated the effects of the full-sun heat. Heading steadily downhill toward the eastern valley, we began to pass ranches with horses and cattle. Basically, the detour was a left, right, right, left to regain the trail. Behind us trailed the last of the Collegiate Peaks, while ahead and to the right lay the next series of 14ers with Mt. Antero appearing first.

Cognizant that we were passing by and through the Princeton Hot Springs resort, an instance of "great minds think alike" occurred. Proceeding down a long curvy road below which the sprawling resort stretched out, my thought process can be summed in three words: "Resort, Restaurant, Food." At an intersection where our detour pointed right, we saw on the left the sign "Lounge, Restaurant." Northern Harrier spoke first—it was apparent what was on his mind although he controlled his zeal for a second breakfast admirably:

Northern Harrier (casually): "Want to see if they're open for breakfast?"

Me: (not so casually): "Of course!"

We didn't hesitate. A full hearty second breakfast helped sustain us the rest of the day. While awaiting the order, we talked to a vacationing couple from Texas who, like so many others, were fascinated by our hike and asked many questions.

Back on the road, we engaged in a "spirited discussion." Here's the thing about our conversations while hiking: there isn't much. And it's not merely because we're often too many paces apart. When hiking uphill (which we're doing 40% of the time, although some days seem like 90%), conserving one's energy is important. I've known and hiked with people who can carry on a near-normal conversation while ascending 1,000' in a mile. There's even a school of thought, although by no means a consensus, asserting that if you can't do such, then you're not "in shape," your conditioning is inadequate. My immediate response to that latter point is to scratch my head and observe that I've never seen marathoners hold running conversations (pun intended). For my part, the rule is "no talking going uphill." If this means I'm "not in shape," so be it. Northern Harrier goes along with this although much more than me, he's perfectly capable of talking and walking (uphill) at the same time.

So when we're not hiking uphill, what do we talk about? Our conversations are not just confined to the usual "The creek should be in 1.5 miles" or "Those rocks did a number on my left foot." Politics and religion? For us, these subjects are not inherent with the usual friction that causes them to be taboo in pleasant conversation. We're pretty much eye-to-eye on such matters, and any such discussion serves as mutual enlightenment.

But perhaps we needed to argue about something, so when he mentioned the Maine coast where he vacations every year, I put a little burr under his saddle. "The Maine coast is tragic," I posited, "because aside from Acadia National Park, the potential of a potentially-beautiful rock-strewn shoreline is despoiled by beach houses, shops, motels, etc. An unfettered view of the dramatically stunning coastline is nigh impossible because of the human-imposed visual pollution."

"Oh come on! Compare it to the Jersey Shore! Now there's some sprawl!"

"Oh sure, I agree. But compare it to Big Sur or even the California North Coast."

"Maine was developed long before any notions of parks and land conservation, and it was all privately owned. Towns have been there for 200 years. People have vacationed there for 100 years."

"Yes, true, the towns were there—it wasn't pristine like Big Sur still is. But the sprawl wasn't as extensive 50 or 60 years ago when other parks were created. There was still enough land in-between to save, but it didn't happen. On the East Coast, you've got Hatteras, Assateague, Fire Island, and especially Cape Cod. All National Seashores and all protected. They're nice but they're all basically sand. Only Maine has the neat rocky cliffs. It's just unfortunate that none of it was preserved. You can't get an uncluttered view of the coastline without contorting yourself."

"You're overstating—there's lots of nice views and not just at Acadia."

"Just go to Big Sur some time and you'll see what I mean."

About which time conversation drifted off as we left the road and began a steep ascent under mostly full sun. We had just entered Segment 14. The ponderosa pines were "conveniently" spaced such that little shade was available. And this was the pattern for about seven miles until we finally ascended into an area with more ample forest cover. So we didn't fully enjoy these seven miles except for when we looked back at views of Mt. Princeton and other high peaks. Lunch was under the most expansive canopy of shade we could find to shield us from an overexposure of solar energy. Next came a 600' ascent in which we made reasonably good time despite the fact that the treadway was strewn with loose rocks when it wasn't soft sand or gravel. The former wore out our feet, the latter was treacherous on the subsequent descent.

We encountered a few fellow sojourners on this less-than-leisurely Thursday. A mother and son were out for a brief day-hike, as was a couple from Dallas. To the latter pair, the heat we felt was nothing compared to the weeks of 100+ degree temperatures and drought that they'd been suffering through in Texas. That conversation reminded us to not complain about dry heat and low-80s temperatures.

Some concern arose when Four Mile Creek—the creek before the one where we planned to camp—was barely a trickle. Like most nights on this hike, we were counting on camping by a water source and the afternoon was getting late. Fortunately, when we reached our destination of Sand Creek 1.3 miles later, the generous flow was more than adequate to meet our needs. We found it interesting that the name "Sand Creek," along with last night's discouragingly named Dry Creek, were both misnomers. Sandwiched between two ridges, the campsite rested on a knoll like many of its predecessors; not ideal, but adequate. Similar to last night, our tents were pitched on bare dirt sandwiched between aspens and evergreens. Our total of 16.9 miles hiked for the day was a new high.

The string of days without rain ended today. A few drops fell when we first arrived, causing us to delay setting up our tents. Sun re-emerged for a while; up went the tents. Then a larger mass of menacing-looking clouds approached along with thunder. Into the tent went everything while we waited the storm out—something we often did in the first week of the hike.

Although we expected to run into Mike, Austin, and Mickey today, they never appeared. Perhaps they succumbed to the temptations of Princeton Resort? We knew that we'd see them again at some point.

Today we passed the official half-way point of the Colorado Trail. We planned to celebrate in Salida tomorrow. The timing worked out because my boots probably weren't going to make it much further; they were falling apart in several places. Hopefully the Salida outfitter would provide the resolution.

For our last morning before Salida, we indulged in another sleep-in—'til 5:30 am! I realize that "sleep-in" and "5:30 am" are incongruous in the non-hiking world, but not on the trail! Our 6:35 start with an ascent of roughly 500' led to a ridge, after which a steep descent took us down to Squaw Creek. Good thing we hadn't come here for last night's camp. This creek was virtually dry and there were no suitable campsites around. This was another example where the guidebook didn't tell the reader everything. The narrative and the book's table of milepoints listed the two creeks back-to-back with only 2.2 miles and 200' of elevation separating them. So was it not a reasonable conclusion that any up-and-down between them would be minimal? Well no, not in the world of mountain backpacking. Not mentioned in the book was the 500' ascent and descent between them. What about the book's elevation profile? I didn't read it closely enough.

This 500' "bump" may have been enough of a surprise to invoke PEE, but the hike was still enjoyable because (1) the ascent occurred early in the day when we welcomed the warm-up, and (2) the morning sun's rays glowing on the aspens and the rocks were pleasing to the eyes, further affirmation of the benefits from rising and starting early in the day.

The aforementioned ascent plus a 600' climb from the Arkansas River were the only bumps of the day. Arkansas River! Now that's progress! Thinking back to our crossing the South Platte on our second day, I sensed an appreciation of the vastness of the U.S. as exemplified by the nation's major river systems. We now crossed a river that flowed south through Oklahoma and Arkansas where it empties into the Mississippi, well south of Memphis. A mere 18 days had lapsed since crossing a river whose journey took it to the Missouri River near Omaha and subsequently to the Mississippi north of St. Louis. While the distance between the points where these rivers end at the Mississippi is much greater than the span between their headwaters, you still feel a sense of accomplishment at having walked the latter.

Much of the hiking along the flank of Mt. Shavano, another 14er, was not difficult and actually, rather scenic. I didn't know whether it was because we were further south or because of the eastern sun exposure, but Mt. Shavano appeared to be devoid of any snow. Perhaps the western side was different. Trail footing today was mixed: some easy dirt, some rocks, some loose gravel. Hiking a brisk pace as we anticipated the pleasures of a town stop, we had stopped for lunch by Cree Creek when a young hiker came by and introduced himself as Tyler.

"Tyler—are you on WhiteBlaze?"

"Yes."

"I'm Cookerhiker, also on WhiteBlaze."

"Oh, yeah—I remember you."

"I knew you'd catch up."

I recognized his name from the WhiteBlaze.net forum on the Colorado Trail and he recognized mine. He was a youngster (26) and hiking over 18 miles per day. Tyler's plan today was 26 miles (!) and skipping Salida. He wouldn't stop again to re-supply until Creede which, from where we were at the moment, was over 100 miles away. His hike started a week after us but with his pace, I knew it was a matter of time before he'd catch up.

Tyler stopped and snacked during which we enjoyed a nice chat. Tyler was obviously in terrific shape but he struck me as having more than simply the physical ability to backpack in the mountains. His ready smile and positive demeanor, his apparent flexibility at responding to unexpected challenges, his "can do" persona all betrayed the perfect temperament and disposition to thru-hike a long trail like the Colorado Trail or the much-longer AT. I asked him whether he had plans to thru-hike the latter. "I'd like to, but can't get all the time off. That's why I hiked this [Colorado] trail."

Living near Peoria, Illinois, Tyler couldn't visit the AT on weekends, nor was any challenging hike within an easy drive. So how did a denizen of the prairie, miles from any hills let alone mountains, turn out so fit? Long-distance running. I've long thought that with respect to conditioning one's body for a long backpack trip in the mountains, the single most important priority was aerobic fitness. In other words, if you're aerobically fit, you're "in shape." Tyler was another example confirming my theory.

After Tyler went on his way, we finished our lunch and headed on. Yet another descent through open chaparral brought us to Rt. 50 at 12:30 pm. The heavier traffic volume along with the presence of more than one major power line announced that this road was a major crossing, probably the busiest such avenue that the Trail crossed over its entire length.

Ten minutes of hitching from a shoulder smaller than we'd have liked brought no rides until a camper van going the opposite way stopped, did a U-turn, and headed back toward us. I noticed the van's Georgia license plates—could it be Bluebird, the young woman with the dogs we met at the start of Segment 13 hiking up Mt. Yale? Yes! It was a reunion of sorts. I don't know who was more appreciative. We needed a ride and she was out of gas money so we were able to help her on that front. Bluebird was en route to Telluride to check out a job opportunity and almost out of money. She was convinced that divine intervention had brought us together. Who's to say otherwise? Trail Magic from a Trail Angel!

Bluebird gave us door-to-door service to the Simple Lodge & Hostel. Through the luck of good timing, we pulled up just as John, the owner, was returning from an errand on his bicycle. First thing we did was hit the shower—felt so good after seven nights on

the trail—followed by doing laundry. Dinner was at an Italian restaurant on F Street, Salida's main drag.

I instantly took a liking to Salida, characterized by its historic
downtown thriving with local businesses. One such local business
was the outfitter which I visited not just to purchase a new fuel
canister; my boots were definitely shot, falling apart in several
places and would never make it to Durango. Heck, they might not
even make it to the next pass where we rejoined the CDT. So I
bought my first-ever pair of low-cut hiking shoes: Merrills, the
same brand as my now-defunct boots. They felt quite comfortable
while walking around town.

After visiting the public library for internet access followed by
obligatory ice cream, we were back at the hostel where we re-
united with Mickey and her dog, Cassie, whom we had met two
nights ago at the Dry Creek campsite. Mickey and I walked to the
Safeway where I purchased a few items not included in my maildrop. Thus far, all of our maildrops had arrived intact and waiting
for us.

Northern Harrier and I shared a bunkroom with six fellow travelers. As of bedtime, no cancellations for the next night had occurred yet, but John said to keep checking with him. We were the
hostel's first guests to arrive today. Although off the trail and in a
town, "hiker midnight" still prevailed as were also the first guests
to bed. A poor night's sleep ensued, probably caused by the rich
dinner (pasta with cream sauce) and my downing a 20-ounce bottle
of iced tea shortly before bed. Not smart. Except in one respect, it
was smart: we had decided to forgo beer, wine, and other alcohol
pleasures during the course of the hike, even on zero days.
Whether you're hiking or just hanging out, hydration in an arid
climate at high elevation is so important that we didn't wish to take
any chances.

On our first zero day, we took it easy, chatted with fellow hostel guests, went to an arts festival in the city park, enjoyed another
good dinner, and basked in the satisfaction that here on this 13th of

August, three weeks of hiking had brought us 250 miles on this challenging yet beautiful, diverse, and rewarding trail.

Dry Heartland — Salida to Eddiesville Trailhead

"None of us could think of the last time—on any backpack, not just this one—that we were so gratified to see a creek."
Day 25 — August 17, 2011

W HEN YOU'VE HIKED AND camped for three weeks, adaptability ensues. You compromise on standards governing matters whose availability in "normal" everyday life you take for granted. You accept the fact that you have to purify your water rather than simply turning on a faucet. Bathroom needs are satisfied in ways that would horrify your childhood Sunday School teacher. You're wearing the same clothes over and over and don't mind it, just hoping your mother doesn't find out until it's too late. When sustaining the inevitable small injury—perhaps a twisted ankle or a cut drawing blood— you just deal with it without the hygienic niceties of proper sterilization for the latter. You crave food and drink, you fantasize about the ideal meal, but upon reaching town you'll take anything that presents itself. The most conservative hiker broadens his/her concept of what it means to live a "civilized " existence.

So it was that I really didn't mind sleeping on the concrete floor of the Simple Lodge and Hostel's garage, a necessity because all of Saturday night's prospective guests materialized into real guests. Actually, only I had to forfeit my bunk because there was one space freed by a cancellation which I yielded to Northern Harrier in deference to his seniority. And I slept well, aided by about four layers of sleeping pads furnished by John. Would I have had this option at a no-vacancy Hilton? Okay, I don't stay at Hiltons anyway. Would I have had this option at a Ramada? Days Inn?

Northern Harrier, Mickey, and I were up early to partake of breakfast at a pancake house about a mile from the hostel. John

Mickey joins us at Salida. We hiked together for ten days.

and his wife, Julie, were ready to shuttle us at 7:20 am, depositing us on the trail before 8:00. The Colorado Trail's halfway point and our first zero day were behind us; a new phase commenced, one which would further illustrate the Colorado Trail's diversity.

We faced 90 miles until the next resupply. While seeming lightweight (and they were individually), the aggregate effect of seven days worth of meals made my pack quite heavy. Typical dinners were little baggies of various grains, e.g. bulgur wheat, pre-cooked brown rice, whole wheat pasta, and couscous. The routine was to cook these starches first and subsequently add flavor using packets of sauces, chiefly dried cheese, tomato sauce, or ground dry-roasted peanuts. Dried onions and mixed vegetables further enhanced the taste and added nutritional value. Breakfast was a hot cereal concoction involving quick oats, flax meal, spices, and other ingredients accompanied by hot chocolate. Perhaps both Northern Harrier and I were strange (or rather realistic and flexible?) in one regard: although ardent morning coffee drinkers in our everyday lives, we both eschewed it on the trail, not just this hike but all others we had done. For me, the need for calories trumped the caffeine fix, hence my morning libation choice of hot chocolate.

For the most part, the ascent up to the Continental Divide was in accord with the book's elevation profile, steady and gradual until the last mile or so. My new Merrill trail shoes fit perfectly and seemed entirely natural while hiking. The fact that I twisted my ankle on the ascent was a coincidence. Sometimes the paths with the easiest footing are where things like that happen because you get careless. I suppose substituting "I" for "you" is more accurate.

Cloudy skies started the day—as John had remarked, quite unusual for Colorado. Sun broke through for brief cameo appearances, but most of the time the skies remained cloudy. Now cloudy skies here in the Rockies are never the dull, monochrome gray devoid of form and variation that often typifies eastern weather, sometimes for days on end. The clouds' different shades of gray along with the ever-changing patterns are fascinating and, like the wildflowers with their riot of colors, provide entertainment quite different from anything emanating from human-made sources. Sometimes, the "gray" of the clouds took on a bluish tint which heightened the contrast between the "blue" clouds and the gray rock of the mountains.

It's tempting to pick out shapes in the cloud formations: "That looks like a ship!" "Over there, I see a pumpkin." All such patterns are fleeting, replaced by other objects or dissipating into a shapeless mass that doesn't resemble anything you can think of.

108

Perhaps it's inherent in us to match cloud patterns with familiar objects, whether natural (pumpkin) or human-made (ship). It's fun and amusing. On the other hand, I also feel that perhaps it's just better to enjoy the phenomenon for what it is in its own right: a beautiful, creative, and dynamic cloud cover.

Furthermore, a good part of me finds objectionable the instinct to compare any natural observation with some matter constructed

Swirling shades of gray greet us atop the Monarch Crest.

by humans. In 1984 when Keith Davis and I hiked a section of the AT in New Hampshire's White Mountains, our first day was a very steep ascent up to the Presidential Range. We hiked slow and steady on a beautiful sunny day, enjoying a constant breeze strong enough to offset our bodies' sweat and cool us down. Keith averred that this was "...like hiking in air conditioning." I don't recall my exact response, but I recoiled at this comparison. Keith's description was understandable in a sense, but it just didn't seem right to reduce a refreshing mountain breeze in a timeless setting of evergreens, rocky mountains, clean air, blue skies, and sunshine to a human invention less than 100 years old which was designed to negate a different force of nature. If anything, I'd turn things around: "Air conditioning enables us to enjoy the feeling of cool, dry mountain breezes on a hot, humid, sticky day." I suppose it's inevitable that for most of us living in urban/suburban areas surrounded at work and home by modern technology, nature often takes second place in our observations and even our thoughts.

As the hike proceeded and the trail steepened somewhat, we met two northbound section-hikers who assured us that water was plentiful at Marshall Pass, our intended destination for the evening. While talking to them, some mountain bikers appeared, shortly followed by a typical-looking backpacker. Typical-looking, that is, except for the Colorado Trail logo sewn on his blue shirt. He was Bill Manning, Executive Director of the Colorado Trail Foundation.

Well this was a chance encounter! We took advantage of this opportunity to give him feedback about the trail and guidebook, but in a lighthearted and forgiving manner. In my experience, it was highly unusual to encounter the Chief Executive Officer, even that of a large hiking organization, actually out backpacking. It's somewhat equivalent to standing in a Whole Foods checkout line and finding out that the shopper behind you is John Mackey, the Whole Foods, Inc. CEO (incidentally, John Mackey is a hiker who's backpacked the AT). "Hey, glad to see you're not always behind a desk," was my unspoken thought. "By the way, are you aware there are mistakes in the Segment 6 section of the guidebook?" was my spoken thought. "Yes, and there are others as well." was Bill's response in a tone that suggested that he had heard this feedback more than once.

Bill struck us as a very nice guy as he took photos of us, we took photos of him, and he gave us a completion card to turn in when we finished the trail. I surmised that part of his purpose for hiking out here was to personally assess the trail and perhaps advertise the foundation. Subsequently, I learned that he was section hiking the entire trail over several years and would complete it one year later.

We had gotten ahead of Mickey and her dog, Cassie, but they caught up as we were talking with Bill and the mountain bikers. This was the pattern most of the day when we met other hikers later on. Proceeding along, we met more mountain bikers and then two young women backpackers resting by the side. One lived in

Denver, the other—like me, a fellow New Jersey native—currently lived in Houston and had just flown up yesterday to tackle a section-hike of the Colorado Trail. That's sea level to 11,000'! Their names were Audrey and Nicole and both were in good spirits despite being very tired.

The truly steep part to the ridgeline known as Monarch Crest began as we emerged from treeline. No other way to put it: the slope was way too steep with the loose rock and gravel making it highly prone to erosion, as well as rendering the footing difficult if not dangerous. I averred aloud that I couldn't think of any place I had ever hiked that needed switchbacks more than this few hundred yards. But I couldn't run back and tell Bill Manning now! Besides, didn't he just descend this ultra-steep slope an hour or two earlier? I also felt darn glad that we weren't hiking downhill on this terrain. Was I being wimpy or unduly biased or groaning from a state of fatigue? From the guidebook:

> "Begin a climb that ascends 668' in a half-mile, one of the steepest grades on the entire CT." (page 180)

So not surprisingly, it felt good to reach the top where Northern Harrier was waiting along with two more northbound mountain bikers. My immediate thought was, "How are they going to make it down that slope?" And sure enough, their descent was quite tentative and, I imagined, as stressful on their nerves as it was on their brakes.

As Mickey took her final step of ascent, we exchanged a high-five. Some 15 minutes later, Audrey and Nicole trooped up. At this 11,900' elevation, views were marvelous in all directions. But the views also revealed very threatening skies—praiseworthy in their cloud patterns' artistry but threatening nonetheless. We hustled along the ridgeline, planning lunch at one of the few shelters on the Colorado Trail. Reaching the shelter before the onset of sprinkles, we noted that the small size and dirt floor did not exactly enhance its appeal.

The others joined us, along with a German mountain biker named Andre from Dusseldorf. He was biking the entire CDT (which had re-joined the Colorado Trail at Monarch Crest) southbound and only had a week to finish before his flight home. In this regard, Andre was an exception in that nearly all the mountain bikers we had encountered were day-trippers.

During our typical gourmet lunch (bagels, cheese and gorp), the rain began, not hard but steady as we all squeezed along the one thin bench at the shelter's edge. A penetrating chill permeated the air and our bones, probably knocking the temperature down by at least 15 degrees. On went the rain pants and warm hat.

I really admired the two girls' spirits, for despite their slow pace and being tired and cold, they were cheery and positive. In this respect, they set a good example even for veteran hikers like me. While we were huddled in the shelter, they shared their freeze-dried ice cream. Incredulous? There actually is such a treat. I remember indulging in such during the 1970s when I often bought prepared backpacker meals from outfitter stores. This "ice cream" in substance is dry and powdery, unable to be reconstituted to anything resembling the authentic. But the flavor is reminiscent of the real stuff.

Audrey and Nicole also tried to pawn off other vittles, half-joking that they wanted to lighten their packs. I asked innocently if they really needed those bottles of wine but they didn't accept my unsolicited advice to jettison them even though I offered to take one off their hands. Of course I was bluffing. Compared to water, alcohol may be lighter (in weight, not effect!), but it was still excess weight. At least for a long-distance backpack, it's extra weight. As for short hikes, that's a different matter!

By about 3:00 pm, the rain had largely dissipated, prompting Northern Harrier and me to venture out ahead of the others. More scenic, above-treeline hiking preceded the descent into the woods and down to Marshall Pass. Coming to the water source first, we dropped the packs and walked further down to the trailhead parking lot near the official Segment 15 terminus. Finding no ideal campsites, we decided to stake our claims back by the water. The thickly-wooded grove of conifers provided just enough space to fit our tents between the trees. We were joined within the hour by Mickey, Audrey, and Nicole.

As defined by our experience thus far, today was typical in that we hiked 14 miles and camped near a water source. But we knew that starting tomorrow, this "normal" routine would change as we entered the upcoming stretch of water paucity. After reviewing the limited options for the next few days *vis-a-vis* the water situation, bedtime was a later-than-normal 7:30. During a middle-of-the-night foray, I observed a cloud cover over the bright moon with no stars visible. So although the forest never became totally dark, it was gloomy and damp when we began stirring at 4:50 am. For the first time on the hike, visibility at our 6:00 starting time was marginal—barely enough light to see the trail. None of our fellow campers stirred.

Misty, pea soup mornings may be wholly normal in the East and parts of the Pacific Northwest, but it sure seemed very strange to start the day hiking in fog in the Colorado Rockies. Wasn't a bright morning sun the natural order of things here? I enjoyed the opaque atmosphere (kind of) as something different, knowing that it wouldn't likely persist very long, and appreciated the sublime beauty of hiking in the mysterious mistiness. It's easier to appreciate it as long as you're not hiking in it all day, every day! Sure enough, the fog was burned off by 9:30.

I felt nauseous and queasy this morning (why?) but still led on the gentle ascents we covered. Even though much of the morning was in forest, I sensed a hard-to-define difference from the previous segment. It seemed like wide spans of open country surrounded a ribbon of trees through which we walked. We were also hiking a segment in which motorized vehicles (read: jeeps and dirt bikes) were permitted. We saw several of the latter today.

One aspect of today's hike similar to much of the previous segments: rocky footing, especially starting around mid-morning. By day's end, it had become very tiresome for me. I thought about those who complain about the rocks on the Pennsylvania portion of the AT. Those rocks are nothing compared to the Colorado Trail!

After all, it was this morning when the following little incident occurred: We were walking on rounded, mostly loose and small rocks (three inches across) so cluttering the Trail that we couldn't avoid them. A rock stepped on by my right foot launched another rock partially underneath it, tiddlywinks style, directly (sideways) into the inside part of left foot's ankle. Ouch! Now that hadn't happened in my 35 years of hiking, nor would it likely reoccur in the next 30 years. I couldn't replicate that catapult action if I tried.

So there were rocks, not just in the footpath but also in a large talus slope to the right which, fortunately, we didn't have to hike across. Our descent from a high point named Windy Peak was characterized not only by a rocky trail, but also a very dense forest of lodgepole pines. There was no way one could stray off the trail here, for the trees were packed together so tightly that an average-sized person could barely fit between them. Of course, a forest like this one was quite dark in the middle of the day and not surprisingly, no understory of plants,

Can't see the forest for the trees in this stretch amidst dense pines.

bushes, grasses, etc. grew in the few patches of dirt along an otherwise barren, rocky ground The setting prompted me think that whoever coined the phrase "Can't see the forest for the trees" probably hiked right here! If not here literally, it was a very similar such forest.

Tank Seven Creek was our noon target destination, which we reached with three minutes to spare, though not without some anxiety. We were satisfied with our pace of 11.6 miles in six hours over rocky terrain with ups and downs, and my early morning nausea had vanished. The anxiety stemmed from missing some interim points listed in the guidebook, namely a pipeline crossing and the so-called Tank Seven Cut-off, a side trail. We didn't see any pipelines or side trails or signs for such but when we arrived at a decently-flowing creek with very dry-looking country straight ahead, we surmised correctly that this body of water was Tank Seven. A very critical point because Tank Seven was our first, last, and only water source today; we planned a dry camp tonight. Looked like the guidebook needed clarification—more feedback for the Colorado Trail Foundation! At least the creek flowed generously as we cooked hot dinners and filled our bottles and bodies with water while managing a friendly wave at some traversing dirt bike riders.

What followed was 1,300' of ascent spread over 3.6 miles to the end of Segment 16. The extra weight from carrying three full liters of water in my pack along with the half-liter in a pouch affixed to my pack's belt strap caused a lessening of pace. Much of this stretch was in the open and by the time we started, the now-intense sun was shining in full force. Our pace was steady enough that we made decent time while taking short breaks from the heat in the few spots of sparse shade that we came upon. The last portion was Sargent's Mesa where numerous cows were grazing. Reaching it before 3:00 pm, we rested and pushed on into Segment 17. A northbounder had spoken disparagingly about the cows here, but to us their impact was far less bothersome than those encountered in the Lost Creek Meadow on our 5th day.

After a gentle but hot and rocky descent, we hiked our last ascent of the day, a 400' slog up to a ridge. As we subsequently de-

115

scended on a gradual grade, we looked for campsites. By the time we found some fairly level and pine-needled spaces amidst a dense coniferous forest, we estimated based on the book's milepoints and our pace that we had ended at Mile 3.7 of the segment. This meant we had hiked 19.1 miles—the longest day by far. Feelings of satisfaction overcame fatigue, for we were now well-positioned for the next two days in this water-scarce portion of the Colorado Trail. Actually, we felt less tired than many of our shorter mileage days in the hike's first half.

Having finished our cold supper, we were writing our journals around 6:30 when Mickey and Cassie showed up. After two days now, we were still on the same pace or schedule. She found a site a little ahead of us in the same general vicinity.

In my tent tonight, I was greeted by a most unpleasant surprise: a hole in the tent floor behind where my head lay, presumably caused by a mouse or some such other little creature. One way to look at it: I'm sleeping very soundly! No evidence was discernible that it reached my food bag. Perhaps the effort expended from chewing through the tent proved too exhausting. It's ironic; word is that bears aren't usually a "problem" on the Colorado Trail, so unlike my eastern hiking I've rarely hung my food in a "bear bag" strung up and dangling from tree limbs. Obviously, it wasn't just bears we had to worry about. As it turned out, we never saw any sign of bears for the entirety of the hike. But that doesn't mean they weren't out here.

* * * * *

WEATHERWISE, THINGS WERE back to form after the previous night's aberration as a clear cloudless night prevailed with bright stars and near-full moon. But even the moon's glow barely provided sufficient light to hike when we took our first steps a few minutes after 6:00 am. Reluctantly, we decided that this morning would be our last 5 am wake-up. The positive aspect of this morning's darkness was a perfect photo-op featuring the full moon framed by shadowy evergreens forming black shapes against a faintly-brightening dark blue sky. Said picture later constituted the front of my 2011 Christmas card.

We neither saw nor heard Mickey as we trod gingerly in the semi-darkness. Chances were that since she caught up to us yesterday, we'd see her again later today.

We experienced no single 1,000' ascents today. However, there was a sufficient number of steep ups and downs that made for a strenuous hike, especially trying to walk 18 miles on top of yesterday's 19 miles. Our higher-than-normal mileage was driven by the limited water sources in this dry area of the Colorado Trail. After three early morning PUDs which caused us gratitude that we hadn't hiked on further yesterday, we came to the side trail to Baldy Lake, the only reliable water source until day's end. At least the steep descent to fill our water bottles seemed much less than the half-mile it was supposed to be; it took us only eight minutes each way *sans* packs. Baldy Lake was picturesque itself, its blue waters reflecting perfectly the slopes behind it. The area around the lake featured abundant camping possibilities but we were satisfied with our overall plan and didn't regret our dry camp last night. My knee usually jerks to the position "we have to camp near water" and certainly that's Northern Harrier's preference as well. But the adaptability required for hiking in these conditions was winning out—and I didn't mind. As long as we obtained water *somewhere* during the day, we would be fine.

En route to the lake, we met two hikers (looked like a father-son duo) who had camped by the lake last night and were also hiking southbound. Later on, we caught up to them in an open area. In our brief conversation, the young man evinced a positive attitude and was more fit than his older companion. We didn't see them again, but subsequently, we heard from others that their situation was, to say the least, unconventional. It seems that they barely knew each other, having only recently met through a neighbor of

117

one of them. The young man was totally inexperienced, relying on the older man's presumed expertise, an expertise that seemed very limited from our interaction with them. Example: here in the midst of a 50-mile stretch in which water was scarcer than any other portion of the entire trail, they were assuming availability of, and relying on, water sources that were marginal at best. We never heard how things turned out but we hoped for the best. From the conversation, albeit limited, it seemed to me that the younger guy was better prepared in terms of both his physical conditioning and mental attitude.

Moving on, we descended gradually through another open area. In a rare instance where I was about a hundred feet ahead of Northern Harrier, I noticed a man coming in our direction. As we neared each other, I saw that his shirt sported a Colorado Trail logo. I spoke first:

"Hi—are you with the Colorado Trail Foundation?"

"Sort of—I'm a volunteer. Name's Appel."

"Oh, aren't you the Trail Angel at the pass ahead?"

"That's me. I may not be back when you get there. You'll see a tent and canopy set up when you get there. Help yourself. It's two miles before the [CO Rt. 114] road."

I had heard of Bill Appel from a few sources, including the Colorado Trail forum on WhiteBlaze.net and Mags' website. What I didn't realize was that each spring, he also dispensed goodies to aspiring AT thru-hikers in North Carolina near the town of Franklin. It turned out that he and I had probably been standing within a few feet of each other at times and places, including the Franklin April Fools' Day hiker festival which I attended in 2010.

In AT circles, Franklin, NC brings one man's name to mind: Ron Haven, the owner of three motels in Franklin, plus another one in a Georgia town near the AT. Ron enjoys a well-deserved reputation as a "hiker friendly" guy who offers shuttles and helps the Trail Community in immeasurable ways. Ron was also recently elected County Commissioner. When I mentioned his name, Appel readily responded with a friendly, tongue-in-cheek recognition. "Oh yeah, Ron's a great story teller and he knows a lot about the trail, the community, local history, Native Americans. He can tell you about lots of things and some of them happen to be true." I can't say I know Ron really well, but I'm pretty sure he would have chuckled.

Responding to our queries about water, Appel said that we should be able to find some at the boxed-in spring in Segment 19 near Van Tassel gulch, an iffy source mentioned in the guidebook. Others had told us the same thing. Water was not an issue today as we expected to camp tonight by Pine Creek. Tomorrow, however, we faced another 19-mile walk and were thus eager to ascertain the whereabouts and status of all potential water sources.

We thanked him and moved on. By now, the bottom of my left foot was hurting; even the new shoes weren't cushioning me adequately from the rocks. I was doing my best to avoid stepping on them with much pressure, but the length of the day and mileage proved too much. All told, today included eight climbs of various lengths and difficulties. The last three seemed like the hardest with very steep stretches generously laden with rocks. Over the course of the day, our battered feet brought us to encounters with five dirt bikers but no hikers or mountain bikers.

We began counting the minutes to Lujan Pass where Appel's setup awaited us. Reaching it just as threatening rain clouds enveloped the sky, we pinched ourselves to ensure it wasn't a mirage. It wasn't. Bill Appel wasn't there, but we were greeted by a welcoming sign, canopy with chairs around a table, cooler, and tupperware boxes with everything we needed. After indulging in chips, cookies, and drinks (bottled water for me, flavored high fructose corn syrup for Northern Harrier), we relaxed in the chairs for about a half-hour, then resumed the hike with full rain regalia: pack cover, rain jackets, rain pants. All we got for our efforts were sprinkles, notwithstanding the dark skies and occasional thunder. It appeared that the storm was behind us and we were moving away from it.

119

Had we started our hike an hour later this morning, we'd be wet now. Which meant that Mickey, presumably behind us, would bear the brunt of the rain.

After a difficult-enough day thus far, at least the last two miles to the segment end took us along an easy Forest Service road. Providential! Just what my foot needed. Now entering Segment 18 after crossing the paved Rt. 114, we followed the trail, traversing through open grassy areas flanked by slopes of trees. Our goal was 1.7 miles to Pine Creek (a different Pine Creek than Segment 12), a search which proved elusive. We had crossed the grassy area's low point where we expected to see the creek, but nothing doing. After hiking to a point where the Colorado Trail obviously headed into dry hills, we looked back and realized we'd have to find the creek where it presumably meandered through the grass.

Finding a spot on a knoll for our tents under partial pine tree cover, we backtracked and finally noticed where water flowed under a culvert in the lowest grassy spot. Actually, "flowed" is a generous term; "trickled" is more apt. At least the trickle was adequate for us to draw the vital fluid. There's little question in my mind that water is appreciated more when you go to greater lengths to extract it.

Which brings me to another lesson that I've learned in hiking: when you hike back the way you came, whether by design as an out-and-back trip or by circumstances, you may think it's the same experience but literally it's not. You see things going back that you didn't see in the first place and vice versa. A 180-degree change of direction makes a difference. The culvert was not visible the way we came, only on the backtracking (and barely at that). What's important though, is that we had our water for tonight and didn't mind that it was a longer distance than normal from where we pitched our tents; as was always the case, you make do.

Just after 7:00 pm, supper finished, ready for bed at "hiker midnight," and enjoying the tawny gold hues painted by the alpenglow on a nearby ridge, we heard a voice below and saw Mickey coming up the trail. She evidently saw our campsite but we shouted down for her to get water first before coming up our way where a few spots were open for her tent. Unable to discern if she heard us, Northern Harrier loped down to make sure she knew where to go. Upon her arrival, we commiserated on how poor the water situation was at this Pine Creek. As a Pennsylvania native who, like us, has hiked the Black Forest and Susquehannock trails in the state's rural northern tier, Mickey also knew of the better "Pine Creek"—one that flowed generously surrounded by slopes of green forest. But that thought was fleeting and irrelevant. We were in Colorado now! And our water bottles were full.

I've talked a lot about water, especially on this hike of the Dry Heartland. The need for water is obvious. It's water that connects us with those who have gone before us in these mountains: the Native Americans going back millennia, the early European explorers, the mountain men seeking furs, prospectors seeking gold, naturalists curious over new wonders, poets and dreamers drawn to the heights, trail blazers laying down a pathway for what would become the Colorado Trail.

Northern Harrier and I locate water through our 21st Century tools. We consult our guidebook and maps, we inquire of those whom we encounter from the opposite direction, and if we so choose, we can rely on a GPS. So finding water, for us at least, is less of a challenge, easier than it was for our predecessors.

But what we have in common is the appreciation for both the simplicity and the vitality of H_2O. As modern backpackers on a journey of recreation, we may differ in most respects from Ute Indians or early fur traders like Jim Bridger, but I'd like to think that our simple pleasures at savoring the refreshing libation from a mountain stream are identical. What neither 21st century backpackers like Northern Harrier and me nor our predecessors of centuries past do in this setting is to take water for granted. In this regard, we represent a marked contrast to modern denizens of urban/suburban America for whom water is merely a twist of the faucet or a simple purchase at a convenience store. Even when we hike in the more hydrological East, water availability is foremost on our mind: Where will we get it? Can we camp nearby? What kind of source: spring, creek, larger river, lake, pond? Might it be

The Dry Heartland lives up to its name.

stagnant? Contaminated? Or even dried up? We need to concern ourselves with these very fundamental aspects of water for the situation that we're in. By contrast, how many Americans ask "what's the water situation like?" when they contemplate whether to move to a "warm" climate such as Phoenix or Las Vegas? So in these respects, I felt more connected to the mountain trekkers of old than to my fellow citizens of the current age. Water may be (still) cheaper than gold, but which commodity is truly more valuable?

* * * * *

TODAY'S HIKE HAD PUT US over the 300-mile mark. On the whole, we agreed that the hike was going very well, but lately the rocks had caused constant pain on the ball of my left foot. Taking more ginger and even some Ibuprofen (known as "Vitamin I" in hiking circles), which is usually a last resort, I eagerly looked forward to the next day's foot soak in Cochetopa Creek on what we expected would be our last day of hiking in this area of water paucity. And although we planned to hike 19 miles, we anticipated one of our easier days, given the flat-looking elevation profile of Segment 18. Little did we know...

We got out-of-the-box in short order and hiked rather strong and fast on the gentle uphill grade through the dry forest. Last night's campsite was at Mile 1.8 of Segment 18 so when we passed a gate marking Mile 8 in a few hours, a feeling of satisfaction swept through us. I soon forgot this morning's frustration that occurred during the 15 extra minutes it took me trying to extract a recalcitrant tent stake out of the rock-hard ground.

Then we missed a turn.

It's uncertain when we discovered such; it wasn't a sudden "aha!" We were hiking in a steady and steepening uphill which didn't mesh with the book or pocket guide for this nearly "flat" segment. After a steep ascent on an old road in a forest of aspens, we realized with a sickening feeling that we must have gone wrong and turned back. So retracing our errant steps found us at a signed trail junction which we had recalled passing but at this point, we were completely befuddled. Did we come straight up that hill, or from the right side? I remembered this junction, but coming back 180 degrees made everything seem different.

Fortunately, Mickey and Cassie appeared just then from the one direction.

"Dumb question but are you hiking from the campsite? You didn't take some side trail, did you?"

Puzzled expression: "No, I'm just hiking the trail. Up from the campsite."

"So the trail came from there and goes up here?"

Turning around, looking at the junction sign, and consulting the book again, we finally saw where and how we screwed up. But how did/could that happen? I didn't voice this sentiment to Northern Harrier but in my mind, it was quite apparent that for this section at least, I didn't respect the trail.

Another Cookerhiker principle, "Respect the Trail" is a mantra I'd derived years ago after an AT section-hike in Pennsylvania when I experienced the worst fall ever sustained while hiking. Pennsylvania is infamous in AT circles for long stretches of short, pointed, angled rocks which slow hikers down, chew up boots, ("PA—where boots go to die." PA—where maintainers use files to sharpen the rocks at night.") and often cause both pain and frustration. Actually, there are other parts of the AT with similar or tougher rocky footing, but in those locations the rocky stretches accompany steep uphill or downhill treks where the pitch of the slope captures more of the hiker's attention and exertion, than the footing underneath. The Keystone State's rocky terrain thus presents a contrast to rocky northern New England's heart-pumping, lung-aching steep climbs and knee-busting descents. Were it not for its rocks, the AT in Pennsylvania is an easy hike. Except for a single mile with a 1,000' gain climbing out of a gap, there's little elevation change to speak of in the state. Pennsylvania's rocks are thus the only barrier preventing hikers from trotting along at 4 miles per hour.

So having finished a slow, tortuous slog through a typical Pennsylvania rockfield, I had arrived at a dirt path and began striding briskly along a nearly-level treadway. Rockfree. Except it wasn't—a hidden rock, barely protruding 2 inches, intercepted my toe and I went down hard. I was lucky I didn't break my teeth, and lucky that I had sufficient gauze for all the bleeding.

Resuming at a limp, I mused about how I had underestimated and taken for granted that the hike had become "easy" with nothing stopping me, nothing to be concerned about, no prudence required. I really hadn't respected the trail and its nature, that hiking on a pathway in the woods is not the same as walking city streets or country roads or shopping malls (the latter of which I avoid like poison).

From that point on, I told myself to "Respect the Trail," meaning don't underestimate trail conditions, don't overestimate yourself, enjoy the hike on *all* parts of the trail, don't get overconfident, don't take any part of the trail for granted. Not surprisingly, I have no problems respecting the trail when I'm ascending 2,000' in 1.7 miles or descending steep slopes; the lapses are on the "easy" parts and/or the nondescript sections of less-than-spectacular scenery. When I twisted my ankle the first day out of Salida heading up to Monarch Crest, it was along a stretch where the grading and footing were "easy," hence I was careless. Respect the Trail!

For our hike, missing the turn probably cost us over an hour, and worst of all engendered more time in the full sun, hiking on jeep and Forest Service roads in a semi-desert landscape. And to my surprise and consternation, I had developed blisters on the balls of both feet. Northern Harrier theorized that our fast pace this morning, combined with my strong legs, placed undue pressure on my feet. Maybe so, maybe not. It **was** striking how suddenly the blisters appeared after I had hiked over 300 miles with no problems at all.

We hiked with Mickey on and off the rest of the day, sharing a shady lunch spot under a spreading tree a few hundred feet off the road. We were together when we reached what we believed was Van Tassel Gulch, but thoroughly searching the lush-looking grassy areas most likely to yield water proved fruitless, contrary to what we heard from people whom we had met the last two days. Resuming the hike, Northern Harrier eventually got ahead of me well out of sight. The trail led steadily uphill, finally leaving the open semi-desert landscape for an aspen forest. I was tiring and resolved to take a rest even though he was ahead of me. Next ridge: I'm sitting down! And atop that next ridge, he was waiting for me. We had reached mile 5.4 of Segment 19, the highest point for the day at 10,400'.

From here it was an easy downhill to Cochetopa Creek and none too soon for us. Even on this latter foot-friendly stretch, the blisters were annoying. I couldn't wait for a creek soak! Leaving the Forest Service road upon which the trail had been proceeding, we circled around a knob and beheld the creek ahead of us, sparkly and flowing in a grassy valley with trees further up the slopes on either side. Mickey and Cassie joined us in a few minutes.

What a beautiful sight for sore eyes (and sore feet and parched tongues)! Our joy and excitement were palpable after two days of nothing but glorified puddles. None of us could think of the last time—on any backpack, not just this one—that we were so gratified to see a creek. Striding ahead through the grassy surroundings, we wasted no time in splashing our way into the delightful water. I had no camp shoes and the creek's bottom was rocky, but Northern Harrier graciously loaned me his crocs (lightweight plastic sandals) so that I could wash and play.

The nearest trees were further away from the creek and up a steep slope. Northern Harrier and I set up our tents in the open grass. Mickey cooked her dinner but planned to move on for another fraction of a mile to complete a 20-mile day. We had thought of that ourselves, but now that we had a nice campsite, we were staying put. If you count our errant detour, we did our 20 miles! Mickey then changed her plans when

Mickey and Northern Harrier enjoy Cochetopa Creek.

two more hikers appeared: Mike and Austin, who we had met the same night as Mickey one week ago today. After their family visit in Salida, they were behind us, but hiked 24 miles today to arrive here. Obviously, they were also thrilled to see Cochetopa Creek.

We enjoyed each other's company. I took photos of all the hikers including Cassie, whose short legs and small body, not to mention carrying her food in a pack designed for dogs, didn't seem to inhibit her hiking ability at all. The evening alpenglow from the sunset was beautiful, in the sky and everywhere. At dusk in the mountains, even ordinary-looking grass takes on an enchanting glow.

Bedtime was later than usual but we planned on sleeping in the next morning. After three days hiking 19, 18.5, and 19 miles, the long dry stretch was finally over! On our upcoming ascent over the flank of San Luis Peak, we'd find ourselves back into alpine hiking again for the first time in weeks.

Although the night started out warm, it was quite cold during my 11:00 pm foray. Morning greeted us with a beautiful, clear sky—and with frost. Even with a late (for us) 6:00 am get-up time (for which I was grateful), the cold air was penetrating. Like the Lost Creek area where we also had camped in an open, treeless setting, my tent fly was frozen. In struggling to stuff the stiff, nonpliable fly into my tent bag, I noticed that the holes in the bag were increasing in both size and number, causing me to wonder if it would survive the rest of the hike or go the way of my boots.

As usual, Northern Harrier and I were the first starters, even though we were an hour later than normal. We pretty much followed Cochetopa Creek upstream the whole day. The morning hike was easy, i.e. favorable footing and not much elevation gain, and we enjoyed the glimpses ahead of the high peaks, trying to guess which one was San Luis, a 14er. Northern Harrier and Mickey had already decided they wanted to hike the side trail up to "bag" this one but I probably wasn't going to accompany them.

The sun's pleasant warmth enveloped us after less than an hour hiking with the creek off to our right, never far. We eventually crossed it after which the trail steepened considerably for a few hundred yards up to a knoll. There, we came upon a tent whose occupant sat near its entrance. It appeared he had just gotten up and was taking his time leisurely. As we talked, his unleashed dog growled periodically, causing his owner to assure us that he was friendly but zealously protective. Catching a glimpse of Mickey and Cassie making their way up the trail, I headed back to advise

127

her of another dog's presence at which time she secured a leash on Cassie.

Things were harmonious in that the dogs got along. Whew! For now. We continued on, the views ahead becoming more scenic as we neared the higher mountains. In 6.7 miles, we reached the end of Segment 19 and decided that the swiftly-flowing Stewart Creek was an ideal early lunch spot. Mickey had already hiked ahead when we were joined by the hiker we had met earlier. Exchanging names, he went by Hill.* Like me, his trail name incorporated his real name.

Sprawled on the grass, I watched as Northern Harrier rose to his feet and turned in Hill's direction to my right. The dog was to the left. Northern Harrier took a few steps saying something to Hill at which moment—so fast I couldn't react or shout—the dog leaped at my hiking partner with his mouth open and attempted a big bite out of his thigh.

Northern Harrier (understandably startled): "What was that about?"

Hill: "He didn't get any skin."

No he didn't. Luckily. "Another irresponsible selfish dog owner." I thought. So unlike Mickey, who obviously knew how to respectfully handle dogs, and in a very loving manner.

No more words were spoken. The dog settled down. And we moved on. Hill and his dog were behind us. The high-country tundra was ahead of us, beckoning.

---

* I've changed his name

Alpine Again — Eddiesville Trailhead to Molas Pass

"...today's hike was highly rewarding with the above-treeline vistas all day. We were on the longest such stretch of the entire Colorado Trail. Alpine flowers were still profuse."
Day 31 — August 23, 2011

W E WERE ABOUT TO ENTER THE La Garita Wilderness, the fifth of six such designated areas through which the Colorado Trail passed. So in just how remote a location did we find ourselves? "Wilderness" may conjure up images of stark beauty, but the term also sounds pretty forbidding and isolated, especially when compared to its opposite "civilization." Nothing in the guidebook dispelled the notion of remote isolation, as the driving directions from Saguache, the nearest town of mention, occupied nine lines of text. Eddiesville Trailhead, where we now stood after our lunch and invigorating foot soak in Stewart Creek, was more than 76 miles from Saguache. At least 41 of these miles were Forest Service or county roads, none paved. The last 21 miles were described as "...very challenging when wet."

So here we were in this federally-designated Wilderness Area, miles from access to stores, motels, restaurants (even the ubiquitous Subway chain), police stations, schools, churches, lawyers, accountants, and all of the other amenities which most of us need to live a "civilized" existence. Surely, no one would live out here, right? Then why did a rough dirt road lead off to our left to a gate through a fence, beyond which we could see buildings? As it turned out, the object of our eyes was one ranch—an in-holding** in this National Forest—and as we happened by, the owner pulled up in his pickup truck, grateful for Northern Harrier's opening the gate for him. Our pleasant conversation revealed that his ranch was hosting a wedding during the coming weekend. I speculated that the guests and wedding party would have no problem making it here as long as they didn't make the mistake of choosing stretch limousines for the occasion!

Continuing toward the headwaters of Cochetopa Creek, the trail took us up one of the easiest 1,400' ascents I've ever experienced. Usually, I invoke the PEE when the "erroneous expectation" involves tough uphill climbs, but in this case I mis-estimated the *ease* of the ascent. The few steep parts were very brief. Later on at our campsite, all three of us—Northern Harrier, Mickey, and I—looked at each other expressing nearly identical sentiments: "That didn't seem like 1,400' at all."

The afternoon featured more wildlife sightings than usual. Thus far, 330 miles into the hike, our wildlife encounters of the *fauna* variety had been minimal. We had seen a few marmots, the fox over Tenmile Range, and several Western birds including the ubiquitous Clark's Nutcrackers who flitted around as if to say, "Look me, I've got shades of gray too!" Very true! These birds sport the same array of black, white, and gray as mockingbirds, but feature a heavier-looking body. Although limited to the West, they're quite common.

As usual, Northern Harrier was ahead when I saw him stationary, facing me directly and motioning for silence. "Look right!" in a loud whisper. Which I did. And there they were, no more than 25' behind some small shrubbery: mother moose and calf! The

---

**An *in-holding* is a parcel of private land wholly or mostly surrounded by publicly-owned land, in this case Gunnison National Forest, and is usually included in the "authorized" boundaries of the forest or park. Some in-holdings are eventually acquired by the government, but some remain in private hands for generations.

former was a shaggy brown and she stood, so it appeared, a good ten feet taller than us. The calves were obviously small, although they appeared able to stand and walk around easily. Compared to fawns of white-tailed deer, they were quite larger and more robust-looking.

The moose encounter followed two sightings of snakes—about one-half mile apart, both non-poisonous. Only their disparate sizes (one short and skinny, one markedly larger) distinguished them from each other. Each were a medium, monochrome gray (no different shades!) and both moved too swiftly to capture a photo. They were the first and, as it turned out, the last snakes seen.

Trekking up the gradual incline, alternating between open meadows and increasingly-thinning trees, we arrived at the last crossing of Cochetopa Creek at 3:35 pm. We stopped here for our night's camp, finishing off a 14-mile day. Mickey, Mike, and Austin were already there; the latter two were heading up to camp on the saddle just below San Luis Peak,

Back in the alpine country at 12,000'

which they would climb first thing in the morning. Northern Harrier and Mickey also intended to take this side trail the next day as San Luis was the closest the Colorado Trail approached a 14er. With my still-sore feet, I decided to skip this side-climb which meant I'd bask in the luxury of a late sleep.

The campsite was largely in the open and very windy for about an hour-and-a-half, but then things calmed down a bit. An early arrival translates into a longer wait until dinner, although does it

131

have to be that way?   Mickey approached me while I was sitting on the tundra grass enjoying the high-elevation sun:

"Is it too early [4:00] to cook dinner?"

Emphatically: "Yes! We have a rule. We can't start dinner before five!"

Laughing: "I'm cooking two meals. Just doing the first one now."

Did she know that this was a standing joke between Northern Harrier and me?   Often when we've reached camp early, we've hovered over our stoves ready to strike a match when the clock strikes 5:00. No cooking before 5:00, no bedtime before 6:00.

As I've pointed out previously, life on the trail moves along at a different pace than the "real world" of the home, workplace, city, family, and everything else "normal."   But we established our "rule" so that we didn't stray too far from our conditioned habits. Eating dinner before 5:00 pm is just too unseemly in our minds. There are hikers whose personal preference is to hike longer into the evening and eat later than us. And then there are those who only hike a few miles and habitually stop for the day not much later than noon. We all have our practices, habits, and styles. Our fellow trail trekkers would hardly react to our "rule," even if it strays considerably from their preferences. After all, they, and we, are hiking our own hikes.

"Hike Your Own Hike" (HYOH) is an oft-repeated mantra among backpackers. Simply stated, there's no single "right" way to hike; what works for you may not work for me.   Aside from consensus on reasonable limitations (e.g., HYOH doesn't mean you can dump your litter on the trail or cut live trees for firewood), hiking styles and preferences are personal and thus merit respect from your fellow members of the hiking community. Regardless of the different patterns and preferences among long-distance hikers—our idiosyncracies, habits, terminology ("hiker midnight," "PUD")—we share a commonality that sets us apart as non-conformists to civilized norms.

132

After we finished supper, a young thru-hiker came by.

"Room for one more?"

"Of course—come on over!"

Stedman was a fast hiker like Tyler, who we had met just before Salida. With a very light pack, he was hiking 20-25 miles per day. He planned to arise at 3:00 am and hike up San Luis Peak to catch the sunrise. We told him to look for Mike and Austin who by now had moved up the massif to the side trail junction on the saddle.

All told, five of us shared the campsite: Northern Harrier, me, Mickey, Stedman, and Hill who had joined us before Stedman's arrival. At least his dog and Cassie seemed to get along and no incidents arose between dogs and/or people. Hill mentioned that he was a trail maintainer participating in many of the Colorado Trail Foundation's work trips. In that regard, I have to applaud him despite his temperamental dog.

At 11,755', I expected another cold night—perhaps another frost? I looked forward to savoring my sleep-in the next morning while Northern Harrier and Mickey would rise earlier for their San Luis climb. Adding to my appreciation of the late start was my poor night's sleep. Listening to Northern Harrier and Mickey getting ready for their earlier departure, I felt the sun's rays warming up the scene. When I finally emerged, only Hill's tent was still standing. Never heard Stedman who presumably stole away in the wee hours.

The morning was cold but manageable, likely a few degrees warmer than if I had arisen at the normal 5:30 am. I was more than half-way through morning chores when Hill began stirring. Departing at 7:30, I hiked the 1.2 miles and 850' ascent to our rendezvous at the San Luis side trail in 46 minutes. Even considering my normal early morning strength, this pace told me I'd become a much stronger hiker in nearly four weeks of trekking this trail. I sat down in the tundra grass at the saddle to wait and began to cool down rapidly at this 12,600' elevation. Backpacks belonging to

Northern Harrier and Mickey lay at the junction, but there was no sign of Mike and Austin. Presumably, they had already climbed the 14er and moved on.

For at least a half-hour, I gazed at the mountain not seeing anyone. It was about 9:00 when I saw two dark figures perched and prominent on what appeared to be the top. Northern Harrier and Mickey's forms became more recognizable as they inched their way down, bettering the estimate of 9:30 with two minutes to spare. By the time they arrived, Hill had passed by. After Northern Harrier and Mickey rested, we started down the other side of the massif. All of today's hike was above treeline with stunning vistas of mountains, meadows, and colorful gray skies (not an oxymoron!) in all directions. The flowers weren't quite as prolific as a few weeks ago, but impressive nonetheless. It was no surprise that they were past their peak at this 12,000' elevation on the 19th of August.

This being the Colorado Trail, the descent to San Luis Pass wasn't all downhill and of course there were no level stretches. But the alpine setting made the entire traverse enjoyable. My only problem was that descents exacerbated the blister pain, a pain which quite evidently wasn't going away any time soon. I imbibed in Vitamin I regularly now, something I normally eschew.

We passed Hill before the 500' final ascent to another saddle. Reaching San Luis Pass, it was time for Phase II today, which made us more nervous than hiking any of the Colorado

Nearing San Luis Pass in the tundra.

Trail's 482 miles: getting ourselves to Creede. The town was 10 miles away, not on a highway but via a side trail, four-wheel-drive-only road, and Forest Service road. In other words, this was a **long** 10 miles! Now the time had come for our reliance on a "faith factor," counting that someone out for a spin in their jeep or similar vehicle would take pity on us and offer a ride on this weekday. At least it was still early in the day.

Starting the side trail, the good news wasn't just that the trail was easy and well-marked; it also appeared to be less than the 1.5 miles per the guidebook. Reaching the four-wheel-drive road after a walk of only a half-hour, a single parked car was all we saw of civilization. We began following the road downhill, a most unpleasant walk as we navigated ruts and potholes on the hard-packed surface. The full sun was beating on us and already we missed the cooler temperatures and occasional breezes of the delightful mountain ridges.

After some confusion at a left fork which led to an active mine, we stayed to the right on the road which actually veered uphill. PEE! This was supposed to be all downhill! The only car passing us came from the opposite direction; the occupants promised us a ride on their return trip, but only if they changed their planned return route from the loop drive that they intended.

We were in a funk at the prospect of a long dusty walk. Mickey expressed misgivings at not continuing on to the next segment which ended at a paved state highway 15 miles later, but this crossing was over 30 miles from Creede and had been described in several sources as a "tough hitch." Continuing on the Colorado Trail would also have entailed hiking and camping along a high-elevation ridge exposing us to afternoon thunderstorms. As we walked, the sighting of another moose cow and calf in the road was nice, but did little to boost our spirits.

The road came to another junction with the other side of the mine road. We stopped and munched on snacks. Of course we still had to get to Creede, but thinking ahead I voiced an idea that had just occurred to me in the last hour:

"Keith, I was thinking—now this is just brainstorming, haven't thought it all the way through, but eventually we'll get to Creede. The next segment [No. 21 to Spring Creek Pass] is about 15 miles and ends at a state highway. If we can find people in Creede who offer shuttles and can take us back up here, what about staying two nights and slackpacking Segment 21 tomorrow?"

Another "great minds think alike" moment: The words were hardly out of my mouth when Mickey jumped on it: "I was thinking the same thing!"

Some backpackers frown on slackpacking, but fortunately it was apparent that Mickey was not one of them. "The three of us can share the shuttle costs. We could try hitching back from Spring Creek Pass tomorrow or maybe get a shuttle both ways." Northern Harrier was convinced. Now if we can only get to Creede...

Coming up the road toward us were two all-terrain vehicles followed closely by a car with Texas plates driving very slowly. As they neared, we noticed that the ATV drivers were very young-looking women. We stuck our thumbs out and the car, after going about a hundred feet past us, backed up, rolled down the window, and asked where we were going.

"We're thru-hiking the Colorado Trail—it runs up there along the ridges. We've hiked 90 miles since our last town stop and need a ride into Creede for supplies and rest. We'd appreciate any distance you can take us, just a mile or two would be great."

"We can take you to the parking area down by the junction. It's only about a mile-and-a-half but another road comes in so you may have more luck getting a ride there."

The family was on a vacation and the girls driving the ATVs were their nieces. They were turning back by the mine road anyway and returning to the aforementioned junction where they would drive up the other road. As we rode along, the couple asked us a lot of questions about our hike and seemed very interested and impressed. Before we got to the junction where they were to drop

136

us off, the husband offered to take us all the way to Creede! Trail Magic had struck again! "You all are true Trail Angels!" we told them. Dropping his wife and nieces off at a picnic area, the husband took us all the way down a rough, steep, and slow road to Creede, depositing us in front of Kip's Restaurant. He refused our offer of gas money. We thanked him profusely, still marveling at our good fortune as he drove away.

After feasting on burgers at Kip's, we checked in to Bruce's Lodge where Mickey managed to get the last room that accommodated pets. The situation was the exact reverse of Salida where she had reservations for two nights and we didn't. This time, we had the reservations and she was only confirmed for this first night; the motel was booked solid for the following night. We ran into Mike and Austin, greeting them with both hello and goodby since they were heading back to the trailhead this afternoon and continuing on. They were running out of time in which to finish the hike to Durango.

Next up was arranging shuttles. We learned of a woman named Debbie who could shuttle us back from Spring Creek Pass tomorrow afternoon and return us there the following morning. Mickey called her for arrangements while I discovered that the owner of San Juan Sports, the local outfitter, possessed a four-wheel-drive vehicle to shuttle us to the side trail that we had hiked down from San Luis Pass.

So we were set! Feeling jubilant! Back at the motel, I talked for a while with four older couples, at least they were older than me or so I thought. Like so many others we had met, they expressed fascination with our hike, asking numerous questions. And like similar previous encounters, I enjoyed talking to them and must admit that conversations like this do wonders for morale, not to mention ego. Perhaps when you hear your voice describing what you've done and what lies ahead, you acquire a further appreciation of the enterprise. You're reminded that backpacking 480 miles over rugged mountainous terrain is impressive by most of society's standards for physical undertakings. Yes, all we're doing is walking. We don't need the skills and coordination required to play 18 holes of golf or hit a tennis ball into a small quadrant. But a hike like this brings about its own challenges, both physical and mental, and it's gratifying to hear firsthand others' heartfelt interest and admiration for our feat.

Creede was the smallest of all our overnight "urban" stops. I found it remarkable that this modest community included a good outfitter. Mickey acquired a new rain jacket and I bought a fuel canister and Aqua Mira water treatment drops. Northern Harrier and I had been sharing mine ever since his Aqua Mira bottles developed a pinhole. Also, we decided that it was more efficient to share my stove for the remainder of the hike. The town's grocery store was a more-than-adequate source for supplies, including moleskin for my blisters.

But Creede's restaurant choices were limited. Dinner was at a local Mexican restaurant, the quality of which disappointed both Northern Harrier and me. And Kip's, site of our lunch, may have been the only eating establishment in the whole USA whose menu featured hamburgers but no French fries. No fries! Such an omission borders on negligence, especially for hungry backpackers.

Another restaurant was situated across the street from the motel but didn't open until 7:00 am, so we availed ourselves of the grocery store to stock up on breakfast food for tomorrow's early start. On the other hand, the coffee espresso cafe in Creede was a cool place. Best of all, the cafe served homemade ice cream. The maple-flavored variety was out of this world! That's more like it! In Cookerhiker's ranking, ice cream merits a higher priority than French fries. The woman behind the counter who dispensed the frosty delight was the proprieter of this fine establishment. She reminded me of a friend back in Frostburg, MD, where I lived for 2 ½ years, and who coincidentally was also a small business owner.

* * * * *

138

ON THE DAY MARKING OUR FOURTH week trekking the Colorado Trail, we reveled in a fabulous hike! The lighter load on our backs from slackpacking this difficult segment made all the difference. Michael McNeil, our shuttler, was the owner of San Juan Sports. Our early start enabled him to return to the store well before opening time. A transplanted Okie native who had recently moved up from Texas, Michael and his wife had just bought the business last year. He drove us up the road where the old abandoned mines once flourished at a time when Creede and other now-defunct towns flowed with people, money, and minerals.

It took the three of us (well, four counting Cassie) 33 minutes to hike up the side trail to San Luis Pass on this beautiful blue-sky morning. Ready to start at the trailhead, I noticed a hand-written sign taped to the signpost reading:

No Slack Packing
NFS
Mike and Austin

We enjoyed a good laugh out of that and mused over what we'd say if we ever caught up to them again; perhaps "Your sign would have been more believable if you had said 'USFS,'" was my thought. We probably wouldn't see them again but you never know. Mike and Austin were very strong hikers, but usually started an hour or more later than us so perhaps they were somewhere up the looming slope, watching us laugh at their sign.

Speaking of "looming slope," right off-the-bat we faced a 1,000' ascent in only 1.3 miles up to a saddle. This became the pattern for the first half of the day: rising to a saddle, down again, sometimes in trees briefly but usually in tundra above treeline. Starting from about halfway through Segment 20 the day before yesterday, we had finally returned to the "real Colorado," with sweeping vistas of mountains, passes, and gorges, all while tramp-

139

ing on alpine meadows underfoot. Snowy peaks glimmered in the distance. This was what I had originally expected hiking the Colorado Trail. It was hard to look down while hiking (a more-than-occasional necessity as the trail was still rocky in places) because my eyes kept wandering to take in the views. Even though the ups were strenuous and the downs painful and requiring attention, today was an enjoyable and rewarding experience. Our pace for the day's first half was less than what we needed to meet our shuttle, but we expected to accelerate as the terrain's undulations became gentler.

After reaching the highest saddle at 12,785', the next feature was the long descent to Snow Mesa which was not as flat as something called "mesa" would imply. More indicators of the alpine: we passed a colony of pika (small rodents resembling chipmunks but endemic to high mountain climates) and followed a marmot down the trail. The descent to the mesa included two manifestly unpleasant stretches through rockfields where a single misstep could sprain an ankle or worse. Surrounded by talus slopes, these trail conditions were unavoidable. However, most of the trail was in fine shape. Once again, I marveled at how well the Colorado Trail Foundation marshaled a dedicated cadre of volunteers to build and maintain the trail in such a remote location.

By the time we first strode onto Snow Mesa, what had become a predominantly cloudy sky afforded only a few scattered openings for sun; another day of typical Rocky Mountain weather was upon us. After a fast lunch by an unnamed lake, we hurried along the mesa which featured a rolling up-and-down landscape. As the sky became totally overcast, it also became even more enchanting. Much of the West is "big sky" country, but it seemed that Snow Mesa's broad expanse revealed more of the sky before us than our views along the other above-treeline stretches. And from a larger, grander sky came an even greater variety of gray colors and cloud patterns. Distant clouds which likely yielded rain were discernible in more than one location, separated from each other by other patterns.

We knew that it was raining somewhere. Would our time come? Would it reach us? Would we hike into it? Our time did come, about two-thirds of the way along the mesa. Fortunately, no thunder or lightning developed. All three of us donned our rain gear, but like most of our experience to-date, the rain was more of a steady drizzle than a heavy soaker.

More shades of gray as storm clouds envelope Snow Mesa.

The descent off the mesa was initially rocky but more forgiving as we reached treeline and viewed our destination below, the highway at Spring Creek Pass. As we approached the road, nearly an hour before our scheduled pickup time, Northern Harrier caught a glimpse of two hikers near the privy in the trailhead parking lot. Mike and Austin! Unbelievably, we had caught up to them. They had started late this morning after camping at San Luis Pass. In fact, as I had surmised they had seen us from the saddle above San Luis Pass when we started this morning. They also spotted us above them as they were trekking on Snow Mesa. Our reunion lasted for about 45 minutes until they moved on. As the rain continued, we stayed relatively dry under a thick conifer while awaiting our shuttle from Debbie.

It never came. By 5:30 pm, a half-hour after the appointment, we realized that something was amiss. Adding to our consternation, there was no cell phone service at the pass, not even for Mickey's "smart" phone. So we began hitching. Actually, Mickey and Cassie did the thumbing and the reasons were obvious notwithstanding political incorrectness: like it or not, it's easier for a woman to hitch a ride than two guys. The odds increase even more when it's a woman with a small dog. Of course, women hiking alone run more of a safety risk on many fronts, but that wasn't an issue here *per se* since we were all together. Northern Harrier and I merely remained about 100 feet back in the parking lot.

A truck stopped and two guys heading to the Rio Grande Reservoir drove us about halfway to Creede. At the road junction where they turned off, another car we flagged could only take one of us, and no dogs, so Northern Harrier went, taking with him Debbie's phone number to determine her whereabouts. About ten minutes later, Mickey and I succeeded in persuading an elderly couple—ranchers from Nebraska—to take us into Creede. It was on their way. We may have been the first, and possibly the last, hitchhikers they ever picked up. I enjoyed a nice conversation and learned a lot about ranching. For their part, they appeared unable to comprehend why anybody would voluntarily strap 35 pounds on their back and walk in the wilderness. The ride proved to be a "teachable moment" for all parties! By the time we reached Creede, their initial apprehension had abated somewhat, but I'd still be surprised if they made a habit of picking up hitchhikers. To say that there was a culture gap is a gross understatement! But nonetheless, they attained the status of Trail Angels whether they knew it or not.

At dinner in the restaurant across the street from the motel, Debbie, our would-be shuttler came in, and found us. She profusely apologized for, in her own words, "screwing up." That's okay! Over the course of a long hike, things go wrong sometimes. Debbie still planned to shuttle us tomorrow when we'd resume the hike from Spring Creek Pass. This time we expected no "screwups."

Our motel was still full, but the owners generously allowed Mickey to pitch her tent in the backyard where she and Cassie spent the night.

As the day ended, my reflections included again how our progress could be measured by considering the major rivers that we had encountered. We had crossed the Platte on our second day, we had crossed the Arkansas just before Salida (and saw the river in town near the hostel), and now we were in the Rio Grande watershed. I looked forward to hearing the reactions of friends in Texas when I told them, "I was at the Rio Grande this summer."

Early the following morning, we partook of a full breakfast at the crowded restaurant across the street. Debbie appeared right on time, taking us to the beginning of Segment 22 at Spring Creek Pass where our hike began shortly before 10:00 am. Along with the later-than-usual start, we faced a tight water situation in the upcoming segment. For those reasons, we planned to only hike 8.5 miles for the day. Our destination was a grassy meadow where water presumably flowed. This stopping point would put us in good stead for the next day's ascent to the Colorado Trail's highest point.

Unlike many eastern trails, the Colorado Trail features very few shelters. We had taken refuge from a downpour at the small dirt-floor wooden structure on the Monarch Crest on our first day out of Salida. Some reservation-only backcountry huts were also present near the trail back near Leadville, but we didn't avail ourselves of them. No shelters of any kind were mentioned in the guidebook's Segment 22 chapter. However, Mickey and some other hikers had told us of a yurt* somewhere around the meadow where we planned to camp. I opined that it was probably locked and required reservations like other lodges earlier on the trail. My perception was that its main clientele probably consisted of winter cross-country skiers.

The trail proceeded through open country and along roads only accessible by jeeps and similar vehicles. These types of roads rare-

---

* A yurt is a domed, circular shaped structure of soft material used as a shelter. Its historical origins date back to ancient Central Asian peoples.

ly appeared in the hike's first half, but their frequency had increased in the past week since leaving Marshall Pass. Invariably, these jeep roads were replete with deep ruts and dips as well as loose gravel. They're not pleasant to walk on. Keeping our eyes and attention on the rough ground more than usual, it was hardly surprising that we missed a turnoff. Northern Harrier and I had no clue when Mickey suddenly called out "hold on." Studying the GPS application on her sophisticated smart phone, she realized that we were off-course. Turning around, we retraced our steps until we found the correct direction. Thanks to her, our errant wandering probably amounted to less than a half-mile.

Most of the day's trek was uphill but rarely steep. After a few miles, we hiked up Jarosa Mesa, a very gradual ascent. At the crest was a horrendous rockfield requiring slow and gentle steps—not exactly helpful to my blisters. The gently rolling, nearly level landscape on which we found ourselves belied the fact that we now stood higher than 12,000'.

Approaching a meadow stretched out before us, we couldn't find the expected water sources. But after noticing the yurt up a slope to the right, we searched more intensely until we spotted a few pools in the lush, green grass. Although the water wasn't exactly a fountain of delight like Cochetopa, we made do (as always), remarking that it was easier to extract than the second Pine Creek. On my knee in the grass, I dunked the water bottles in a shallow pool and topped them off using my cup as a ladle.

The threatening clouds had somewhat dissipated as Northern Harrier and I considered tenting under the trees shortly beyond the meadow. But the yurt was unlocked and apparently available. One look at the inside convinced me to stay: bunks with pads on springs, chairs, tables, stove, sink, nice deck. Sure, it was somewhat warm inside but temperatures cooled down later, especially when the rain clouds again began to envelop the sky. I apologized to Mickey for my pessimism about the yurt's accessibility.

We had been joined during the day by Jacob, a young south-bound CDT thru-hiker who also hiked the AT in 2009, grew up in Columbia, SC, and presently lived in Portland, OR. He kept saying he was going to hike on another 20 miles but evidently he liked the yurt and/or our company; he ended up staying. We were later joined by two CDT northbound section-hikers Erin and Chris. Upon finishing their current hike atop Monarch Crest before Rt. 50, they would officially become Triple Crowners. They met on the PCT and were getting married soon. Chris hailed from Cornwall, England.

Despite the banter of conversation from the younger set in the yurt, I easily drifted off to sleep, but later awoke as the rain splattered noisily on the roof. I was very glad we had decided to stay here rather than move on and tent.

* * * * *

WHEN YOU'RE CAMPED IN close proximity to fellow hikers, simple common courtesy is appreciated all around. This applies to those of us, like Northern Harrier and me, who habitually rise before the others. As a compromise to our norm, we emerged from the sleeping bags at 6:00 am, instead of the usual 5:30. The original intent was to leave promptly and defer cooking breakfast until further along the Trail. But we didn't relish setting up on the wet grass which was still soaked from the previous night's rain. Remaining in the yurt, we moved as quietly as possible to pack and prepare breakfast using the yurt's stove.

As was typical, another spectacular sunny day in the Colorado Rockies greeted us in the early morning. Feeling quite strong this morning, I led for the first hour up a very steep incline through an evergreen forest. Eventually, the trail rose above treeline and emerged into the open, revealing splendid vistas everywhere.

Northern Harrier's words rang out loud and clear: "Fantastic! I just love that!"

The object of Northern Harrier's expression of *amour* lay downward into the valleys and canyons where fog nestled thickly,

High above the fog-shrouded valleys.

presenting a stark contrast to the blue skies and sunshine where we now stood. On a hike like this, so many features, so many settings will enchant the hiker, be it colorful flowers, clear skies, snowy slopes in the distance (and some up-close), flitting birds, fresh air, or the sensation of seeing distant points miles away. Often, it's all of the above. This time, it was standing on a sunny high mountain ridge and gazing down at fog-shrouded valleys. We've experienced this phenomenon on other hikes, notably Vermont's Long Trail, and it was present again this morning. Northern Harrier couldn't get enough of it, and I thoroughly enjoyed seeing him so captivated. I also marveled that we were probably 1,500' above those valleys, but enjoying drier and warmer temperatures!

A day of ridge and saddle ascent and descent culminated in the highest point of the entire Colorado Trail at 13,271', which we reached at about 11:30. No more elevation-related breathing problems! The steepest climb of the morning was prior to the high point, taking us to the 13,000' level. Thinking back to our first week, I remembered gazing up at Mt. Guyot from Georgia Pass. Guyot's snow-capped peak had seemed so high then, and yet now, we enjoyed our lunch while sitting in the grass at nearly the same elevation as Guyot's summit.

Looking back the way we had come, we saw Mickey and Jacob in the distance. Jacob caught up quickly and didn't linger too long. Mickey appeared while we were still relaxing in the grass at the high point, which ironically appeared in a "flat" area. One might expect that a hike up to the highest point on a 486-mile trail in the Colorado Rockies would culminate in a dramatic, steep hand-over-hand climb, but that was not the case.

In addition to stupendous views along the rolling tundra, we were lucky to spot three ptarmigan by the side of the trail. What a find! I'm not as keen a bird watcher as Northern Harrier, but I still marveled at my first sighting of these fowl-like inhabitants of the tundra. Their camouflaged colors worked perfectly; only their movement betrayed them. Movement is also what pika do, and we saw plenty of them scampering about throughout the day.

The Colorado Trail's highest point appears in a "flat" area.

Our hike to the end of Segment 22 was along a jeep road involving a 1,000' descent in 1.5 miles, sometimes on the road, sometimes parallel. Arriving at a crossroad, we turned right up a steep incline to the beginning of Segment 23. Here was another example of "road access" for which the guidebook description includes:

"...This is not a road for the squeamish. It is very steep, rocky, and narrow, with many tight switchbacks and some significant exposure..."

Anyone who considers starting or completing a hike at this segment transition should be cognizant of what it takes to reach this point by vehicle. And yet, despite this difficult accessibility, other people were around. Some ATVs passed by while we rested where the trail turned off the road. Later, we were to meet other hikers.

Our target for the evening was a small, unnamed lake about 5.5 miles into Segment 23. Ahead of us came one more 1,000' ascent along the Lost Trail Creek drainage to a saddle before we'd descend to the lake. Early in the hike on Day 4, we "discovered" Lost Creek. Now, we'd come upon Lost Trail Creek. Presumably, it's the trail that's "lost," not the creek which, though out of sight, likely flowed in the cleft down to our left. So for us, at least, "Lost Trail" was never found, hence the name is still valid.

I seemed to hit a wall in the afternoon. I found the ascent very tiring and challenging while Northern Harrier, as usual, was well ahead. Frustration seeped in; after four weeks on this trail, why did I still struggle on some uphills? Being near 13,000' again, perhaps high elevation was still affecting me after all. Or perhaps it was just late afternoon blahs after extensive up-and-down earlier in the day. Northern Harrier provided encouragement, saying that we were both hiking very strongly, and in the larger scheme of things, he was right. Just because some days are painful doesn't mean that the hike's not going well. And my inability to keep up with him was as much a tribute to his increased strength as any weakness on my part. I admit that I felt better when Mickey caught up to me near the ridgetop; before any words came out, the look in her eyes told me that her feelings about this ascent were similar to mine. Her words confirmed it: "That was a tough one."

At about the two-thirds point of the ascent, I caught up to a middle-aged couple whose binoculars were trained down the slope to the left. Before I even reached arm's length, the man practically shoved them into my hands.

"Down there, a pair of moose. Here, have a look."

I usually catch my breath pretty fast, but not on this ascent. "Can't see them, my eyes are fogging up from sweat. Sorry, but thanks."

"So you're from Kentucky? Live in Lexington?" Northern Harrier had evidently passed this tidbit on to them.

"Yeah—what about you?"

"We live in Northern Virginia now, but..." He pointed to his blue University of Kentucky cap, which I hadn't even noticed. "Went to college there."

"Oh. Well, I used to live in the DC area."

"So you root for the Wildcats?"

"Nope—only moved there two years ago. Still a Terps [University of Maryland Terrapins] fan."

"Have you hiked the Appalachian Trail?"

"Yes, I've hiked the whole trail."

"What year did you hike it?"

I'm afraid my annoyance showed: "I didn't say I *thru*-hiked it. I said I've *hiked* the whole trail."

"Oh, what year did you finish?"

"05—hiked 700 miles that year. Finished all my missing pieces up and down the trail in a bunch of section-hikes. Saved Katahdin [the 5,267' peak marking the AT's northern terminus] for last."

" I did it in ..."

I couldn't remember what year he said, but it was some time in the 1970s. They were in a talkative mood but I felt weary and besides, I wanted to catch up to Northern Harrier. I wished them happy trails and moved on.

When we encounter passersby in "normal," that is, off-trail life, we don't usually greet one another, let alone strike up conversations, unless it's with people we know. On hikes, it's just the opposite: no one fails to at least say "hi" and acknowledge the other person. More often than not on the trail, a conversation ensues.

Although we hadn't seen a lot of fellow trail users, the trail was not empty and we did engage with most that we did meet.

So I didn't like that I was short with him because all he wanted was some friendly, innocuous conversation. It wasn't like I had ignored or brushed past him, but I probably didn't come across as pleasant. Undoubtedly contributing to my demeanor was my reaction to his presumption that "hiking the AT" was one-and-the-same as "thru-hiking the AT." Since I regard thru-hiking the AT as an awesome and forbidding challenge, perhaps I should have been flattered that he thought I was capable of such. But I'm sensitive, perhaps overly so, to any notion that there's a single "right" way to hike a long trail, a notion that's implicit in the question, "What year did you hike it?" The fact is, the overwhelming majority of hikers on the AT at any given time are **not** thru-hikers.

Typical afternoon clouds covered most of the sky with only little bursts of sunshine penetrating slightly. Mickey had caught up to us, and as the three of us were descending to the lake (a descent in which I slipped and fell on the gravel), the temperatures plummeted, and rain commenced, quickly transitioning to hail. The little white balls bounced on the ground, on our packs, and on our bodies. Swirling cloud patterns gave the sky more of a hodge-podge look than usual. By the time we reached the lake, conditions had actually reverted to sunshine. But only over our heads; a glance back up the mountain where we had just hiked revealed a landscape white from the hail. What a difference a thousand feet of elevation made! Also, the unmistakable rumbling of distant thunder boomed, but we never saw any lightning.

Our reprieve of sunlight was brief. So what else is new? After we found nice sites for tenting near the lake and cooked early, i.e. pre-5 pm (against our "rules"), the threatening sky brought a cold rain which struck while I was still eating dinner. I finished eating in my tent vestibule. I had also discovered an unpleasant surprise; apparently I had left my bag of grains (couscous, quinoa, rice) back at the yurt. At least I could cook the sauces and soak them with my extra bagels. The bagel supply was just sufficient enough to eat dinner this way until arriving at Silverton, which, at 30 miles, lay two days and one night away. We resolved to make big miles tomorrow so that we wouldn't reach Silverton too late on the following day. By now, we had decided to take our second zero day in Silverton.

Camped at over 12,000', I wondered: how could this *not* be our coldest night? It probably was; we arose amid what felt like temperatures in the mid-20s.

The heavy frost again stiffened my tent fly, preventing me from stuffing it into the increasingly hole-ridden Mountain Hardwear tent bag. All I could do was wrap up the tent and fly into a shapeless mass and strap it on the pack in the usual place. Stuffing the sleeping bag into the pack was also a chore, but

A cold but beautiful campsite

a morning like this made me grateful for bringing the 15 degree-rated bag instead of my very lightweight and compact bag used for late spring and summer camping.

Freezing, non-functional fingers and a cold body don't sound enjoyable but they didn't prevent me from savoring the exquisite morning light. The lake's mirror-still water perfectly reflected the ridges glowing from the faint rays of the predawn sky. As we started hiking (uphill of course), we soon passed into the sunshine, ushering in a palpable warmth. A colorful patch of blooming flowers provided a different kind of warmth, the kind that comes from buoyed spirits and morale when observing Nature's beauty. Before long, we encountered a fellow backpacker sitting by his tent in the now-full sun. "Yeah, I saw you guys down by the lake but I knew

I'd get the morning sun first up here. It may be higher, but it's warmer." So true, so true.

On the one hand, today's hike was highly rewarding with the above-treeline vistas all day. We were hiking on the longest such stretch of the entire Colorado Trail. Although not as numerous or widespread as they were in Segments 6-8 three weeks ago, alpine flowers were still profuse. Wildlife sightings included more ptarmigan, but the prize came in the morning's first half when sounds and movement ahead and to the right caught our attention. A faint rumbling became louder, almost like the sound of horses. And then we spotted them: elk. We watched in fascination as a herd crossed a not-too-distant ridge. I counted at least 30 of the large ungulates tromping up-slope in an orderly procession before disappearing over the other side. It is true that many mammals flock together, often for safety from predators. But deer, sheep, and bison are more spread-out and seemingly random as they traverse the range together. Why is it that only elk, apparently, march in such a structure, with a leader setting the pace ahead of columns of two? It was almost military precision. While sighting elk is not rare or unusual in the Rocky Mountains (indeed, they're a "nuisance" in Denver's western suburbs), encountering them in their natural element was a thrill. As I told Northern Harrier, the only other sighting that would make this hike complete on the wildlife front was bighorn sheep. Unfortunately, the only photo of the elk that I was able to snap turned out blurry.

On the other hand, this morning was very tiring with constant up and down. Like yesterday morning, I was discouraged that I still struggled at times on the ascents but, also like yesterday, Northern Harrier assured me that we were doing fine—making the miles at an impressive pace overall. I just thought that I'd enjoy the vistas even more if there was a bit less huffing and puffing. At times I wondered if our schedule was too ambitious in trying to make Silverton by the next day. And then there's my pack weight, a factor Northern Harrier reminded me of frequently. Without question, a lighter pack makes a difference. The question is, at what cost? Mine is not the heaviest among hikers out here, but I could go lighter if I wanted to invest another $1,000 to replace the pack itself, my cold-weather sleeping bag, and my tent. Notwithstanding the holes in the latter, all three pieces were in perfect working order.

Mickey caught up to us as we lunched at Stony Pass, the dividing line between Segments 23 and 24. We had hiked 10.6 miles of constant up-and-down in less than six hours. "You know," I thought to myself, "that's not bad at all." Like yesterday, maybe my funk's origin was comparing my pace to that of Northern Harrier to a fault.

After lunch for some reason, I caught fire on the next stretch and began striding with a burst of energy I hadn't felt in days. A rolling terrain less abrupt in its peaks and valleys undoubtedly made walking easier, but something else was at work. Taking the lead, widening the distance from Northern Harrier and Mickey, I wondered: where did this come from? How could I feel bone-weary in the morning—normally my stronger time—and feel so reinvigorated in the afternoon?

I don't necessarily consider backpacking as an athletic sport but when regarding professionals in basketball or golf or bowling or tennis or baseball (especially pitchers in the latter), why do even the most elite have good days and bad days, or even good moments and bad moments? In short, what explains inconsistency? Or perhaps I have turned the question upside-down; the real question is why we don't accept and tolerate "inconsistency" more? Is it because over 150 years of industrialization followed by the computer age inculcate us with the desirability of the "normalcy" of sameness, uniformity, homogeneity? We're taught (with validity) that our bodies are machines. Does that mean that if only we can design the right formulae of nutrition, exercise, lifestyle, and other "rules and regulations," we can produce a human body/machine yielding a specific, desired result of uniformity, akin to an auto built on an assembly line or an Apple computer? Won't there always be a "human element?"

Bringing it back to this hike, it's a given that Northern Harrier is (usually) a stronger hiker than me. Why am I usually stronger in the morning? And why is this pattern violated on some days? On the morning we hiked to Breckenridge, it was Northern Harrier who unaccountably displayed a burst of energy and strength, atypical of his norm, when he swiftly strode up that first hill right out of the campsite. Now it was me, hiking very vigorously after lunch, in the afternoon, when I'm usually sluggish. So our "norm" is disrupted some times. Who knows why?

Whatever curiosity I felt about this subject was not enough to burden the mind while I paused by some small lakes, not far from where the Colorado Trail and CDT split for the final time. As my two companions caught up, Northern Harrier's facial expression presaged his words: "What got into you?" The look on Mickey's face was only slightly less astonished as I mumbled "I don't know—I just felt strong and kept going."

Harebells brighten the trail.

I was bemused to see lots of little fish swimming around in one of the ponds as I drew water. They're pretty hardy at 12,500'! A few other hikers lounged nearby, including a young couple we had briefly met in Creede who were also thru-hiking the Colorado Trail southbound. Their names were Stephen and Leigh and they decided to camp here by the lakes. They had taken a zero day in Creede, but we knew they'd eventually catch up to us with their super light packs and the energy of youth.

Like most days lately, the perfectly clear morning sky had become entirely overcast by 1:00 pm. Sprinkles were now steady enough to warrant mounting the pack covers. After leaving the lakes and the CDT turnoff, one more steep, steady uphill was conquered before arriving at the point where we began a 3,000' descent into Elk Creek Canyon—the most extreme such descent of the entire Colorado Trail. The steep initial phase was ameliorated by very frequent switchbacks forming an exaggerated "Z" pattern like I had never seen except in pictures.

Also, Elk Creek Canyon was narrower by far than any descent (or ascent for that matter) of this hike. In that sense, it was similar to canyons in the Southwest which reminded me again of our progress; after all, we were heading southwest, right? Shortly after the "Z" switchbacks ended, we crossed Elk Creek, the first of many such crossings, and the footing became more difficult with wet rocks, loose gravel, and a steep terrain, all of which we navigated while the light rain still fell. So our pace was slow, we were tired after more than 17 miles, and flat places to camp were scarce. But up a knoll sat an abandoned miner's cabin along with sufficiently-level surrounding ground for our tents. For Northern Harrier and me, the day's hike was complete.

Temperatures had also noticeably dropped and, being at 11,775', Mickey decided to hike on another 1.5 miles, and another 1,000' of descent, to a spot depicted in the guidebook where a pine grove would offer better camping and the possibility of warmer temperatures at the lower elevation. Despite the obvious appeal of such a setting, Northern Harrier and I had decided we were finished for the day, especially when considering the wet trail conditions. So for the first night since Salida ten days ago, we camped separately from Mickey, telling each other we'd catch up in Silverton.

I was glad we had stopped here. Even though light drizzle still dripped while I set up the tent, the old cabin's roof was sufficiently functional to keep the inside dry, relieving us from cooking dinner in the rain. The only trick was maneuvering around the floor with its loose boards and occasionally protruding nails. The rain ended at about 6:30 and the re-emerging sun was powerful enough to dry my tent nicely—another advantage of western hiking. The sun also produced a gorgeous orange alpenglow on the cliffs across the canyon, just one more enchanting scene.

So a cold, wet, weary arrival had given way to a beautiful evening with a brilliant, flame-orange alpenglow radiating on Elk Creek Canyon's sheer walls. And another reason for basking with satisfaction: as of today, we had whittled our remaining miles to Durango down to double digits. Isn't 100 miles still a long way to hike? When you first start a hike, 100 miles *does* seem like a long stretch ahead of you, almost out of reach. At the point where you've attained nearly 400 miles under your belt/boots, 100 miles is just around the corner.

I hoped tonight wouldn't be quite as cold as last night while noting that we were still camped at a pretty high elevation.

* * * * *

WE HAD ALREADY DECIDED to take a zero day in Silverton. Having less than 13 miles to Molas Pass with its expected easy access to Silverton, we slept in until 6:00 am. My sleep quality was adversely affected by drinking a liter of cold tea too close to bedtime. Throughout the hike, Northern Harrier had periodically offered me "iced" tea powder; at two tablespoons for a liter of water, it was highly concentrated and highly tasty. Too good, in fact; I drank too much.

Elk Creek Canyon was lovely to behold when the early morning sun shone on the impressive walls, giving the surface a bright orange tinge. Seeing this spectacle was another reason for being glad that we camped here last night. However, Elk Creek Canyon was *not* lovely to walk down, especially the first mile. **Steep!** And tricky, with all the loose rocks and gravel. The trail's condition ratified our decision not to hike further last night with our end-of-the-day fatigue. We thought of Mickey hiking down that steep, wet, and slippery slope late yesterday afternoon and hoped that she had avoided any mishaps.

One reward for the tough early descent was a one-mile stretch through a pine and spruce for-est for which I'm tempted to use the "e" word: it was easy! Probably the easiest mile of the entire hike as our feet enjoyed a flat and relatively smooth surface, very atypical of the Colorado Trail. During this part we met a middle-aged couple hiking north on a thru-hike. They told us how to find water seeps in Segment 27, a valuable piece of information for that anticipated long dry stretch ahead. I felt so satis-fied knowing that we were 5-6 days from completion vs. their status of another month of hik-ing. Interesting—both sported

A pleasant stretch approaching the Animas River

external frame packs, something one doesn't see around too much these days. Perhaps they're making a comeback. My two external frame packs from the 1970s and 80s were hanging on pegs in my shed back home. If I ever want to "go retro" on a backpacking trip, they're waiting for me!

Even though we were following the increasingly wider Elk Creek downstream, the overall steepness of the terrain resulted in four PUDs such that our descent incorporated several small ascents. While they probably didn't amount to more than 300' collectively, I voiced how they consumed energy needed for the afternoon's 2,000' ascent. We snacked at a pond where we observed ducks swimming about. Then it was on to the Animas River.

As the trail finally bottomed out, we crossed the tracks of the Durango-Silverton Railroad. Originally built in 1881 to serve the mines, the train still operated daily, reinvented as a tourist route between the two towns. There is actually an official stop at the Colorado Trail intersection that likely serves not thru-hikers like us as much as weekenders out to hike up Elk Creek Canyon or the Grenadier Range in the Weminuche Wilderness, the southernmost of the six Wilderness Areas crossed by the trail.

Even on a Wednesday, others shared the trail with us. I suppose the canyon made a popular day-hike. Conversational encounters included a backpacking couple by the bridge over the Animas River, a guy out for a few days in the Weminuche Wilderness, and a woman on a day-hike who passed us while we were eating lunch. Crossing the Animas, a tributary of the San Juan River, meant we were clearly west of the Divide for the hike's duration.

Shortly after crossing the river, a long (expected) ascent commenced. We both felt strong and commented how the trail's grading on this section made the climb seem less strenuous than others. By contrast, an ascent up the part we came down this morning in Elk Creek Canyon would have been a killer. But again I wondered: I knew this ascent was coming up, I knew it was 2,000' so mentally, I was ready, indeed psyched. What if it had been a surprise? PEE!

I continued upward when Northern Harrier paused to photograph the train whose whistle proclaimed its pending appearance. Our lunch stop was partway up as the now-gray skies became more threatening with claps of thunder. By the time most of the ascent was complete as we climbed beyond the trees into open country, the rain commenced—probably the heaviest we had experienced

158

thus far while actually hiking. On the way we met Dan, another young northbound thru-hiker. At one point we huddled under a thick spreading conifer while the rain was at its heaviest. We left this "shelter" when the rain diminished, but thunder still boomed.

The last part to Molas Pass was through open meadow at times alternating with forests. Although we could clearly see the road (U.S. Rt. 550), the trail wound its way circuitously for nearly a mile until we finally touched concrete. Within five minutes, we secured a ride from a firefighter, a retiree from the National Park Service, on his way to help fight a fire in Wyoming. A young northbound thru-hiker joined us but wasn't staying in town. What seemed strange was that prior to today, we had only met two northbound thru-hikers: one near Kenosha Pass, one at Tennessee Pass near Leadville. Today alone we met four. Maybe the waning hiking season in this last week of August inspired procrastinators to get going? I rued that these hikers would miss most of the alpine wildflowers. To me, it would have been a monumental loss to forgo those splashes of color which had so enriched our hike, and whose images now occupied the memory card in my camera. I wondered if they had any regrets about forgoing the show of colors or, for that matter, whether the thought even crossed their minds.

After we alighted at the Silverton Hostel's door, Rob, the hostel owner, gave us a private room with two beds and offered to do our laundry (a service not usually rendered) because the town's only laundromat was defunct. Relaxing at the hostel brought more conversation with other guests, all middle-aged motorcycle guys and all friendly.

We learned that Mickey was lodged in a motel down the street rather than here. Sign of the times: we didn't see her, but while checking e-mail and Facebook at the town library's computer, we contacted each other and learned that she decided not to take a zero day in Silverton so she was leaving tomorrow. This would put her a day ahead of us and meant we wouldn't likely see her or Cassie again.

A scrumptious dinner at Handlebar's (recommended by our firefighting driver) was topped off by a brownie sundae dessert. One can indulge in such a shameless mound of decadence when hiking 480 miles up and down the Rockies. According to the scale in the hostel, my weight loss now stood at 30 pounds! Couldn't be! Or could it?

As good as the dinners have been in the towns, particularly Salida and now in Silverton, we continued to abstain from alcohol even before zero days. This was another reason to look forward to Durango where a pub reportedly offered a free locally-brewed libation to anyone who's completed a Colorado Trail thru-hike. We resolved to learn more about this one.

On our zero day in Silverton, I phoned my daughter Alicia one day before her 30th birthday to wish her a happy one and see how things were going as she began her graduate studies at Tulane University. Back at the hostel, Stephen and Leigh, the young couple we had first met in Creede, checked in joined by Dan, Leigh's dad. Dan planned to hike with them on the final stretch to Durango. They had arranged a shuttle for 7:00 tomorrow morning with enough space for us to ride with them and split the costs. Like us, they preferred an early start. No Silverton restaurant opened early enough for breakfast in time for us to meet the shuttle. However, since the hostel's amenities included a self-service kitchen, we procured eggs and other breakfast food from a grocery store in town.

Having only five more days of hiking from this, our last town stop, we had logistics to arrange. Northern Harrier talked to his friend Tom Downing, a Denver resident who had offered to pick us up in Durango next Tuesday. I phoned my former EPA colleague Kelcey Land to arrange a get-together for Wednesday afternoon in Denver. Kelcey and her family happened to also live in Evergreen, so they would then drive me to Keith Davis's house where I'd pick up my car.

Exhilaration was building. The calendar read Thursday, August 25, 2011. In 33 days (two of which were zero days), we had hiked 408 miles with 74 more to go. We had hiked in high elevation tundra, dense forests, dry semi-desert, up and down mountains—most of which were quite steep and/or rocky. We had persevered through hot sun in midday, frosty cold in early mornings, rains of varying intensity up to and including hail, and long stretches with limited water. Our bodies were fit. In short, we had met both physical and mental challenges.

Already we felt a sense of accomplishment. And also confidence. Durango awaited.

A Southwestern Feel — Molas Pass to Durango

*"...before long, the trail seemed to enter a new phase—redder soil
and rocks giving it a more Southwestern look. In general, it reminded me of the Mesa Verde area"*
Day 34 — August 26, 2011

I FIRST NOTICED THE TRANSITION back in the prior segment when starting the descent into Elk Creek Canyon. We
had hiked other steep descents (as well as ascents) but the
scene here seemed different, especially when early evening and
morning alpenglow illuminated the sheer rock walls. I thought to
myself: "Southern Utah. Northern New Mexico. Arizona. Another
sign of progress: we're practically in the Southwest."

And at Molas Pass as we started our final 74 miles at 7:20 am,
before long the trail seemed to enter a new phase—redder soil and
rocks, giving it a more Southwestern look. In general, it reminded
me of the Mesa Verde area. There was still lush growth with sunflowers, Indian paintbrush, asters, and corn lilies. But most noticeable was that the trail was less rocky; only in a few places at the
higher elevation did a few rock-strewn stretches appear.

We began as a fivesome. Early in the morning, all five of
us—Stephen, Leigh, Dan, Northern Harrier, and me—had managed
to squeeze by and around each other in the hostel's kitchen while
cooking breakfast. Ready for our shuttle by 7:00 am, we met our
driver, a young woman who originally hailed from Pennsylvania
and, like so many others, found a new life in the Rockies. She pos-
tulated that this last phase to Durango was particularly scenic and

Corn lilies begin to appear more frequently.

less prone to rain, that we had entered a drier portion of the Colorado Trail. Yet one more sign that we were now in the Southwest.

Today's hike took us uphill for a net gain of 1,600' to a unnamed saddle below Rolling Mountain, followed by four miles to Cascade Creek where we planned to spend the night. The trail ascended very gradually, but not without some intermittent descents. Only the final half-mile to the saddle was steep. The first 8-9 miles seemed to fly by as we maintained a steady pace, likely a tribute to the rejuvenating effects of a zero day as well as our trail-hardiness accumulated from hiking more than a month.

Typical for the hike nearly every day, the sunny morning was giving way to a cloudy late morning. For today at least, any thoughts that hiking this far south would give us reprieves from rain were dashed. Just before reaching the saddle, rain and hail forced us to don our rain gear as we ate an early lunch. After eating, we continued up the saddle amid the heaviest precipitation we had experienced on the entire hike thus far. Usually the rains began at 1:00 pm at the earliest, often later, but not today. Even though we reached our high point on this open ridgeline before noon, that wasn't soon enough. Booming thunder reverberated, although I didn't see any lightning. I elected not to put on my rain pants, but ended up regretting that decision.

Under these conditions, absolutely no time was taken for photos or looking around atop the 12,500' saddle. We couldn't see much anyway and the cameras were packed away. In most places, the trail had become a river as we descended down the rocky slope. Impromptu rivulets in normally-dry streambeds crossed the trail such that a few fords were necessary. Before long my feet were soaked through, but they weren't as uncomfortable as my frozen hands.

Northern Harrier's advice: "Put your gloves on!"

"It's not going to help now. Hands are already frozen. Gloves will just get wet and be useless."

"They'll still give you insulation"

"Once my hands are frozen, they won't help at all, until it stops raining. That's the way my hands are."

For whatever reasons my fingers, starting with the two index fingers, are very susceptible to frostbite. They've been known to turn white in damp conditions even when temperatures are in the 50s. It's just something I've had to live with. However, I suppose having better gloves than my thin fleece pair would have helped. Nothing could be done now except putting things in perspective: the rain would eventually end, we'd arrive at a campsite, cook a hot meal, sleep in a warm bag, and my hands would warm up.

We forded a raging tributary of Cascade Creek, the color of which resembled a root beer float. The rain had stopped but everything was wet. In spite of the sun's valiant effort to break through, skies remained predominantly cloudy. Crossing a bridge over Cascade Creek, we decided to move on because it was still relatively early in the day. While hiking in wet conditions might be uncomfortable, it does not necessarily slow you down; sometimes, you actually hike longer and faster because you're less likely to pause for views, photos, snacks, long lunches, etc. Before long though, we observed some inviting campsites partially protected under spruces, a consideration in case the rain should resume. So we stopped for the night. As it turned out, hiking 15 miles for the day was the exact pace we needed to reach Durango in five days.

Later in the afternoon, two section-hikers also enroute to Durango passed by our site and continued on. We did not see the threesome with whom we started today and to us, it was no mystery. Obviously Stephen and Leigh had the capability to, and did, hike 20+ miles daily but having recently flown from Pennsylvania, Dan likely wasn't acclimated to levels exceeding 12,000'. We hoped to see them again but didn't know if we would.

The sun never exposed itself. All we could settle for was occasional patches of blue sky. Raindrops kept falling sporadically until we went to bed at another early "hiker midnight." Supper was cooked and eaten in light drizzle. But all was satisfactory; after all, we were warm and dry in our tents, the heaviest of the rain was apparently gone (an exercise in wishful thinking perhaps?), and less than 60 miles remained. Today's experience in the heavy rain also exemplified how it behooves hikers to carry a set of dry clothes—and to keep them dry. Everyone on the trail wants to carry as light a load as possible, but some items in the backpack are worth their weight. Perhaps not today but on some occasions involving hypothermic conditions, having an extra set of dry clothes can save your life. No exaggeration.

Not surprisingly, the stars were out after midnight and we awoke to clear skies at 5:30 am. Notwithstanding yesterday's dampness, the tent fly was totally dry this morning. I can't explain why but I'll take it! But the same couldn't be said for yesterday's socks as they were still soaking wet. I wore my spare dry pair today and secured the wet ones on the outside of my pack where the Rocky Mountain sun functioned as my drying machine.

Parts of the trail, especially in the first few miles, were still virtual streams from yesterday's rain. But at least crossing the creek near our campsite (our water source) was a rock-hop this morning in contrast to yesterday afternoon when a traverse would have liberally bathed our shoes and feet. Footing today was generally rockier. The lush growth in the first few miles suggested that this area receives a lot of rain. A few patches of snow lay protected from the sun's rays in areas of forest dominated by Douglas firs.

Six miles of scenic up-and-down under clear skies brought us to the end of Segment 25. Although Segment 26 appears flat on the elevation profile chart, it was actually up-and-down with three good-sized ascents: one in late morning, one up to Mile 4.1, and the final strenuous climb to Black Hawk Pass. Mile for mile, this segment was one of the most scenic of the entire Colorado Trail. It seemed like we had constant views of mountains on both sides as we either slabbed the sides or walked on top of a narrow ridge. Off to the left in the distance, the high jagged peaks of the San Juan range filled the horizon.

A single harebell spike brightens up a talus slope.

Looking at the distant clouds this morning, I had cynically predicted that today's rain would start an hour earlier than yesterday, putting it at 11:00. We did get rain of course, but I was off by two hours as it commenced around 1:00. At least this time, the rain gods restrained themselves until after our lunch break. Unfortunately as was the case yesterday, we timed our highest ascent, Black Hawk Pass, around when the rain and thunder were the strongest. So we didn't linger at the top of that pass either, but hurried down before any lightning developed. Happily, this day's rain was much less intense than what we endured the day before. The fast-changing, creative cloud patterns in the sky indicated that the weather systems seemed to be swift-moving.

Being a Saturday, we met a few other hikers as well as several mountain bikers, including two near the top of Black Hawk Pass. One hiker was section hiking northbound from Durango to Creede and reassured us of the availability of water at Mile 12.3 in the middle of supposedly-dry Segment 27. Water at this location was something we were counting on for the next day.

Today's water sources although plentiful on the whole, were mismatched. A more-than-ample morning supply from frequent stream and creek crossings gave way to drier afternoon conditions after Black Hawk Pass. The last reliable water before our entry into mostly-dry Segment 27 was Straight Creek. I'm not altogether certain that the sobriquet was valid—nothing is "straight" in the Rocky Mountains—but I suppose it's all relative! Throughout this hike on most nights, we had camped adjacent to or very close to creeks. Camping at Straight Creek would complete a near-15 mile day but it proved untenable. The terrain was much too steep and rocky for tenting anywhere within a reasonable radius. We faced only one choice here. Another dry camp for the night was now in the works, one more instance of the flexibility needed when back-packing long distances. Filling water into all of our bottles as well as our bodies, we hiked on further until reaching Mile 10 of the segment where some very nice campsites under pine trees awaited us. The sun emerged for about two hours during which time we dried our stuff and soaked up the rays.

Today's wildlife spotting was limited to one grouse along with hearing the distant howls of a coyote. As our hike wended its way towards completion, so too did the month of August, which meant that wildflowers were definitely past their peak, though some stretches still displayed their colorful beauty. Perhaps we'd see more when we'd finally begin descending below 10,000' in a few days. Yet their increasing scarcity made me appreciate the flow-ers' presence even more. A striking example occurred in the form

167

of harebells rising in a single spike out of a talus slope though which we hiked. Their cobalt-blue hue against the gray backdrops of rocks was a true work of art, one with no admission charge! Well, I suppose the "admission" was strapping on a backpack and hiking many miles uphill to attain the prize.

* * * * *

SO WE HAD DRY-CAMPED, and faced a tenuous water situation for the next day-and-a-half. But this campsite's upside was how the early morning light made the setting one of our most scenic locales to "rise and shine." Our normal overnight abodes near a water source were usually in a valley or cleft of some sort, in which case the sun must emerge over a slope. But atop this narrow ridge in a semi-open atmosphere, we witnessed firsthand the eastern sky's rising sun announcing the start of another glorious morning. The "shine" part of "rise and shine" was quite literal! The early sun's shine in turn made it easier for *us* to shine.

Today was one of our easier days, "easy" being a relative term on the Colorado Trail! Until the last mile, we walked along a ridge with little elevation change as we strode in and out of lush evergreens, taking in views mostly to the east but occasionally westward. More areas of reddish soil again confirmed that we were in the Southwest. Somewhat puzzling was meeting only two mountain bikers and a father/son hiking north even though it was a weekend, normally a

Northern Harrier pauses at ridgetop.

time when you expect more trail aficionados.

We talked for a while with the latter two, whose names were Bob and Mark. Their hike was by design a leisurely pace the length of which was determined not by distance or destination but by time, i.e. how far they'd progress in three weeks. The oft-heard mantra among backpackers "Hike Your Own Hike" certainly applied to them. Bob and Mark had met Mickey yesterday. We were gratified to hear that she was apparently still doing well, one day ahead of us.

Our schedule today was governed by two factors: (1) water availability; and (2) not wanting to traverse the upcoming Indian Trail Ridge in the afternoon. The latter would constitute our last high-elevation, above treeline, 12,000'+ alpine hiking and like all similar such stretches, early morning was the preferred hiking time. As if we hadn't figured that out by now, the guidebook admonished, "The Trail stays above tree line, with no easy means of escape from sudden storms, from mile 15.5 to mile 19.4. Watch the weather patterns before committing to this section."

Combining Segment 26's 2.5 miles from Straight Creek with Segment 27's "officially" dry stretch of 19 miles until Taylor Lake amounted to more than a day's hike between water sources, at least by our normal pace. Now came the time when we hoped that the three different northbound parties that we had met were correct about the spring found 12.3 miles into Segment 27. The guidebook refers to the aforementioned spring as "seasonal." A heavier-than-average snowfall in the winter of 2010-11, along with later-than-average melt time, should lengthen the "season" of this spring, no? We were told to look for it upon passing the sign for a "scenic vista."

The last mile to our goal involved a 500' ascent mostly via switchbacks. Along the way, we passed a marshy area with a few puddles of very muddy water. Our spring will amount to more than this, won't it? Surely, we hoped. We moved on, arriving at the "scenic vista" sign with appealing-looking campsites all around. But no spring was discernible. Apparently it was not in the immediate vicinity, not even in grassy areas which seemed like the kind of low point where water would run.

Taking off the packs and carrying water bottles, we headed further along the trail looking intently.

"Up ahead, that looks like a place." Nope.

"Around that bend—looks like those ridges converge. It's probably there." Nope.

And so it went for about a quarter-mile until we came to a trickle beneath some wet rocks and grasses. Northern Harrier thought it was most accessible on the right side but I found a place on the left where we could perhaps press a cup into the grass sufficiently to draw the water.

But we only brought our one-liter water bottles, not cups. So Northern Harrier began extracting what his bottle would take in while I hiked back to get my cup. Of course since the time was mid-afternoon, the sky was doing its normal thing with gray clouds and distant thunder interspersing with rays of bright sunshine. Grabbing my cup and additional bottles, I started back, looked at the sky, reversed course, and covered both of our packs with the rain covers.

"What took you so long?"

"Look at the sky. If it rains, you'll be glad I did."

But naturally it didn't rain just then; I had guaranteed such by covering the packs. You see if I hadn't, heavy rain would have cascaded like a fire hydrant, soaking us and our possessions. That's how rain happens while backpacking. Trust me, it never fails!

Once again, in order to obtain one of the most vital prerequisites of life, we couldn't simply turn on a faucet, blissfully oblivious to the source of the *agua*. The whole process of extracting the liquid into small cups and pouring it into our bottles can be regarded as painstaking; after all, it was. But the important thing was that at the end of it all, we savored the simple pleasure of having full water bottles and could now enjoy this picturesque campsite.

Sun peeked through again during which time we erected the tents and walked out the side trail to the "scenic vista." This brief stroll was certainly worthwhile. Before us stretched an expansive field of view extending about 300 degrees. It was the gathering and ever-changing grays of the sky that captivated once again: charcoal gray, bluish gray, mockingbird gray, dirty white, some with a mottled look. Nothing was simply "gray."

Back at the campsite, Northern Harrier enjoyed a nap. Our 2:00 pm arrival afforded us plenty of time. And about those gray skies: what would a day on the Colorado Trail be without precipitation? It commenced about 4:00, light but steady. My tent was mostly under a Douglas fir, hence not many drops made their way through. All throughout the forest, we have often noticed dry spots beneath these forest giants and at times, we availed ourselves of the shelter that they afforded. I suppose that if we hadn't found the "spring," we could have collected water droplets by shaking the branches, a task that would have occupied the remainder of the afternoon.

Today's rain wasn't much of an annoyance but I thought back to our shuttler's words that this Silverton-to-Durango stretch was drier. Seemed like the rest of the Colorado Trail to me! This typical afternoon rain confirmed our decision to end the day here at the early hour rather than being caught up on Indian Trail Ridge in a downpour and thus bereft of views, not to mention the risk of being struck by lightening. And like last night's dry campsite, we were situated on a ridge from where we could embrace views (even without trooping to the "scenic vista") and the anticipated morning sun.

The sky never really cleared, so there was no ideal time to cook dinner if we wanted to avoid the risk of a downpour while the stove was roaring. Ever since leaving Salida, we had shared my stove. Northern Harrier usually cooked first since his meal preparation was generally simpler and less time-consuming than mine. After he was finished, I cooked my dried vegetables, bulgur wheat, tuna, and pesto sauce. Rain resumed when the cooking was nearly complete but I was prepared, having stashed the food bag against the Douglas Fir's trunk; everything else was in the tent. In my rain pants and hooded jacket, I sat on a log and enjoyed my dinner in the steady drizzle. Not bad, I thought. At least here on the Colorado Trail, it doesn't rain in the morning. Had I just uttered famous last words I'd regret later? Jinxing our luck?

While preparing for bed around "hiker midnight," I reflected how although I'm not as strong a hiker as Northern Harrier, my pace was quite satisfying along with feelings of being (finally) "in shape." Compared to four weeks ago, I was racing! And looking ahead, only two days and less than 30 miles now separated us from Durango.

Unbelievably, around chronological midnight, thunder roared, lightning flashed, and a steady rain began, heavier and longer than what we sustained during the afternoon and evening. Chagrined, I wondered if this meant we'd wake up to rain or at least to a wet tent. But when we stirred at 5:20 am, the sky was full of stars while light glowed in the eastern horizon. 6:30 found us on the trail.

For our last day above treeline along the Indian Trail Ridge, extensive ups and downs reminded me of Segment 23, although this time the physical strain for me was less of an issue. I was finally seeing the benefits of the increased fitness that comes from hiking over 400 miles. I reveled in my last day of hiking on the rolling tundra, even with soreness developing in the left foot from the small loose rocks. Most of the flowers had waned, including our constant companions on the entire hike, the asters. Perhaps we'd see more when we descended to forested areas, although they'd likely be a different subspecies. The ridgeline wasn't entirely devoid of color, as Indian paintbrush continued to splash its patches of pink in several places.

On a stretch described in the guidebook as a good location to spot elk, we met an elk hunter. I didn't ask such, but wondered if now was the season. August seemed pretty early. He was the only hunter we met on the entire hike and we did not spot any elk down the steep but pretty grassy slopes. Aside from the hunter, no one else shared Indian Trail Ridge with us.

Our strong pace enabled us to make fairly short time along the ascents and descents, most of them steep but picturesque in the open tundra. The highest point took us over the 12,300' level. Coming off the ridge's last peak and taking a left turn to descend to Taylor Lake, I felt a bit sad that we were finished with alpine hiking but also grateful to escape the expected afternoon thunderstorms. Rounding a bend after the left turn, we beheld Taylor Lake—unmistakable and sparkling below us like a jewel.

Taylor Lake was a welcome sight after 22 miles with little water.

After replenishing our water supply and snacking at the lake, it was on to the Kennebec Trailhead marking the beginning of Segment 28, the last one on the Colorado Trail. At Kennebec Pass just before a long descent, we talked to a few guys, one of whom took our picture by the sign where our progress could be measured by one line: "Denver — 450 miles." On the other side of the trailhead parking lot, another sign read "Durango — 26 miles." Just a marathon away!

As easterners having hiked the entire AT, we couldn't help but chuckle at the place name "Kennebec." Some sort of Maine connection? The Kennebec River in northern Maine is the AT's longest river crossing for which no bridge exists. Most hikers avail themselves of a free ferry service provided by the Appalachian Trail Conservancy.

Happiness is a descent which turns out easier than the guidebook description. The first part in particular was supposed to be slow and difficult with a talus slope to inch through. Instead, the trail's pathway was cut through the boulders nicely, leaving only small rocks under our feet along the briefer-than-expected slope. Lunching in shade from some of the occasional trees on the still-steep terrain, we then entered the forest.

The sun beat down fiercely, probably a factor behind the

Durango is just a marathon away from Kennebec Pass.

increasingly-lush growth between the trees as we descended further. Undoubtedly, this understory also benefitted from the normal afternoon rains. But as morning melded into afternoon, no rain came from the few puffy clouds overhead. By contrast, a backward gaze at the barren-looking Indian Trail Ridge revealed a different story as we noticed dark clouds prevailing. At this point, they were not a concern for us as our descent approached the

10,000' point. And as expected, and hoped, we found ourselves among wildflowers again, but different from those in the alpine.

We admired the rock walls present in a few places and marveled at the waterfall tumbling down through Gaines Gulch. For the remainder of the hike, we would follow the watershed of Junction Creek, crossing the creek several times and veering away well out of sight from it at others. Again we were making excellent time on the steady downhill and reached our planned campsite at a bridge over Junction Creek before 2:30 pm. Despite this early hour, there was really no consideration to continue on. This creek crossing provided the last reliable water source for several miles. Moreover, we didn't feel an incentive to hike a longer day today and shorter one tomorrow since Northern Harrier's friend wouldn't arrive in Durango to meet us until late afternoon.

In a physical sense, our last night's campsite on the Colorado Trail was disappointing, belying the book's characterization of the site as "great." Mostly in an open plot with little tree cover on what had become a hot sunny day, I set up my tent sandwiched tightly between low bushes. To avoid sleeping in an oven, I unzipped the fly on both sides and rolled it up to allow cross ventilation. At 8,522', Junction Creek was our lowest elevation campsite since... I forgot when—probably our first week. Even our town nights were spent at higher elevations! Ah, but what a sensuous pleasure to soak the weary feet in the creek! Delightful—just the right temperature, not too cold but refreshing.

Around 4:15, two hikers made their way down the slope. It was Stephen and Leigh, whom we hadn't seen since about a mile past the Molas Pass trailhead outside Silverton. As we speculated, the high altitude was too much for Leigh's dad, so they all hiked back to Silverton where Dan procured a rental car after which the young couple resumed their hike. We had predicted that they'd catch us if this scenario occurred and that's exactly what happened. Yesterday, they hiked a 24-mile day. Better them than me! Stephen and Leigh planned to sleep in tomorrow, but I suspected they'd still beat us to Durango.

My last supper on the trail: whole wheat macaroni, Alfredo sauce, and the remainder of my freeze-dried vegetables. For a preliminary, celebratory act, I indulged in a double hot chocolate for dessert. Typical of the hike since Silverton, we had rain at supper—not much but enough to warrant stashing the near-empty food bag and eat with my raingear on. At least the rain had the good graces to cease before bedtime for our last night.

* * * * *

TO SAY THAT WE WERE excited for this last day of our Colorado Trail hike is a gross understatement. Feeling invincible, we knew that nothing would stop us now, not even a very steep initial 1,000' ascent out of the campsite after crossing Junction Creek at 6:30 am. This ascent's steepness didn't prevent us from reaching the high point four miles later in less than two hours; we were smoking!

Watching the sun rise over the opposite ridge as we headed uphill, we predicted that another scorcher awaited us, but perhaps we'd finish before the intense heat established itself. After the high point, we expected the remainder to be almost all downhill except for a few intervening small PUDs.

More reminders that we were in the Southwest: the stretches of red soil and rocks reminded me of the Grand Canyon when I hiked down from the South Rim in 2003. That is, until the trail took a right turn and looped around a mountain where the soil was more of a gray characteristic of the Northern Rockies. One more shade of gray! At this lower elevation, the lush forest flowers still bloomed, including asters and yellow sunflowers. Continuing to descend, we flushed more grouse. By the time we stopped for an early lunch, we found ourselves in an open forest of piñon pines, junipers and ponderosa pines with their elongated needles—again more southwesternlike. While eating, we dried our tents (wet from last night's dew) in the increasingly intense sun.

Despite being a weekday, we saw a fair amount of others, all either mountain bikers or day-hikers. Our full-sized packs obviously identified us as backpackers. For almost everyone we met and chatted with, the script was nearly the same:

"I see you're out for a few days. Where did you start?"

"At the beginning near Denver. We've been on the trail for over a month."

"Wow, you're almost done. Congratulations!! Say, how many miles is that?"

"A little less than 500."

"Did you spend every night on the trail? Did you carry all your food."

"We stopped in some towns for supplies..."

I told myself as we hiked, met and talked to people, and received their congratulations that this was a day, a moment, that must be savored. We'd hiked 480 miles and now we were almost done. A difficult-to-describe euphoric feeling swept over me in these last few miles, one that by definition would only last one or two hours. This feeling could not be replicated, for it emanated from the experience of what we had done for 38 days. Being inseparable from, and coupled with, the experience, it was a fleeting sentiment. Internalize the feeling, enjoy it while it lasts. Ofttimes in life we, or at least I, fail to fully appreciate momentous events and experiences as they're unfolding, especially those which never occur again in the same form. There will be written words to read, pictures to look at, memories to ponder, none of which replicate the actual experiences and attendant internal feelings.

There are other such examples in my life, such as being present at the birth of my daughters or learning I had passed the CPA exam on my first try. Nothing you subsequently read, no pictures that you re-examine, no after-the-fact conversations that you engage in can re-create the feelings that sweep over you as these pivotal, once-in-a-lifetime events are unfolding. The legendary UCLA basketball coach John Wooden, winner of 10 NCAA titles, always maintained that his greatest, most satisfying experience was winning the first one. For all his celebrations— his subsequent nine titles, his team's 88-game winning streak, his other professional milestones—there could by definition only be one first-time championship. Wooden could never truly relive that moment or feel the exact same way as he did when it occurred. And so with me, there is only one first-time completion of a Colorado Trail thru-hike. I now stood on the threshold.

I guess that it was inevitable on the last day of a long trek: you almost feel guilty that you're focusing on the end, on the hike being completed instead of enjoying this day's hike and the natural features of Colorado's Rocky Mountains as much as any other day. In his popular *Seven Habits of Highly Effective People*, Stephen Covey urges us to "begin with the end in mind." This I did, but not just because I wanted to *be* in Durango; I wanted to *hike* there. For long-distance hiking, the means and end are closely connected if not the same. I suppose it's wanting your cake and eating it too.

At the intersection with the Hoffheins Trail, with less than five miles to go, we held a nice long conversation with three mountain bikers who congratulated us on being nearly done. This chat succinctly capsulized our interactions with mountain bikers throughout the hike, a relationship of mutual respect for each other and for the magnificent Rocky Mountain ecosystem. From them, we also learned that Carver's Pub in Durango was the establishment offering the free beer to Colorado Trail thru-hikers, serving their own locally-brewed ale. While we were in conversation, a middle-aged couple also passed by and extended their congratulations.

After passing Gudy's Rest (like the bridge between Segments 1 and 2, also named for Gudy Gaskill), we reached Junction Creek for the first time in the 11 miles since leaving our campsite. While resting and drawing water, a man named Ernie Norris, whom we had seen a few miles earlier, stopped by and struck up a conversation. Out for a short hike on this pleasant day, Ernie was interested in our hike and also inquired about trail conditions. A genial, retired Midwesterner, Ernie lived in Durango and was active in the Colorado Trail Foundation as a maintainer for Segment 25 and part of Segment 26. He then went ahead of us as we stayed to fill our water bottles for the last time.

The last 2.5 miles proceeded on a steady downhill with a few short ups. When I saw a lizard scampering by, I thought how it seemed so very appropriate, given that the ecosystem here is so different from the 12,000' ridge we had traversed less than 24 hours ago. By now, Northern Harrier's long strides placed him far ahead of me as the trail proceeded alongside Junction Creek for its final stretch.

Thinking the end should be nigh, I stopped for one last look at the guidebook, thinking I may have missed a turn. A woman with a dog who had been leapfrogging me assured me that the trailhead was just ahead. She also congratulated me on finishing the Colorado Trail. More day-hikers out for short strolls were coming by as well. Whenever asked how far I'd come, and answering, "All the way from near Denver," I'd bask in the proffered congratulations. Again, what a feeling! It may have been "just walking" as one of my acquaintances from the AT constantly avers, but right then I felt like the "walking" was bouncing on air.

At 12:45 pm, the trailhead was now in sight, getting closer, closer. And then, there was Northern Harrier, Ernie, and Dan (Leigh's dad) all pointing cameras at me to capture the final steps. Ernie expressed regret that there was no brass band. Hey, no problem! Wow, this was something! I'll never forget the sight of that "reception," of those three guys with their cameras pointing at me as if I had completed an ultramarathon.

Well, I guess I did.

The guys took photos of us at the trailhead sign. I joked to Dan that we had seen Leigh and Stephen on the trail and had blown past them, but the truth was that they had simply enjoyed a sleep-in. "See you at Carver's!" we told him. And for a final act of Trail Magic, Ernie Norris drove us the 3.5 miles into Durango, dropping us off in front of Carver's. Yes indeed, their Colorado Trail Nut Brown Ale was excellent! So too were the bison burger, fries, and other accouterments. As ex-

482 miles behind us as we've reached Durango - time to celebrate!

pected, Stephen, Leigh, and Dan popped by so we had our last conversation with them before leaving.

By the time we had finished eating, Northern Harrier's friend Tom Downing had arrived. Their friendship extended back to junior high days when they both ran cross-country growing up in Toms River, New Jersey. Tom's offer to pick us up in Durango was exceedingly generous. He and his wife Linda left their Denver home at 7 am, so in effect, they were devoting two full days to help us.

We checked into a local motel and completed the normal trail town activities, notably laundry and shower, before hitting the streets of Durango's charming historic district. After walking around downtown and browsing through the local shops, we returned to Carver's for dinner. With several appealing-looking restaurants to choose from, we again opted for Carver's, not just for the free beer but because we liked everything about the establishment: the food, the atmosphere, the ambiance. This time, Northern Harrier and I ordered dessert. Our thru-hiker appetite wasn't leaving us right away!

* * * * *

WEDNESDAY MORNING AUGUST 31ˢᵗ dawned—our first day other than the two "zeros" that found us not hiking. Instead, we were getting in a car for an all-day drive. Reaching the Denver area by 4:00 pm, Tom dropped me off at a light-rail station where I boarded a train to downtown Denver. After strolling around (and procuring some gelato of course!), I found my way to the EPA building and by prearrangement met Kelcey Land, with whom I had worked during the last 15 years of my EPA career. It was nice to reminisce and catch up with Kelcey and to meet her husband David and daughter Kaylin for dinner. The Lands live in Evergreen, so they were able to drive me to Keith Davis's house where I spent the night while Northern Harrier was spending the night with the Downings.

Wednesday's drive from Durango to Denver had been a dress rehearsal of sorts for the "back-to-the-real-world" confinements of the 1,200-mile return drive to Lexington. The "tin-box-on-wheels" was a rude awakening for two guys accustomed to the fresh air and freedom inherent with hiking in the high mountains. When the temperatures hit 100° in Kansas, Missouri, and Southern Illinois, a sense of *deja vu* swept through us as we recalled how the July 21-23 drive westward was equally oppressive in the nation's heartland. Just one more reminder of the benefits accrued from spending 38 days in the Colorado Rockies. But any negativity was transient and insignificant as we still basked in the glow of having hiked 482 miles while looking forward to subsequent adventures in our lives.

Post-Hike

Reflections on the Experience

"The hills not only take [us] away from a complex mode of existence, but teach]us] to be happy [that] it is only necessary to have food, a shelter, and warmth...And so from the hills we return refreshed in body, in mind, and in spirit to grapple anew with life's problems. For a while, we have lived simply, wisely, and happily;..."

Francis Sydney Smythe

I N HIS BEST-SELLING *A Walk in the Woods: Rediscovering America on the Appalachian Trail*, author Bill Bryson describes how many would-be thru-hikers jettisoned their planned AT hike practically at the outset because the trail "...wasn't what they expected." Along with his hiking partner, Bryson himself was to experience this sentiment. The degree to which our expectations confine us varies. Many of my expectations for this hike did not come to fruition *exactly* as foreseen. Such exactitude on my part was not warranted.

I've already acknowledged that mental preparation for a long-distance hike is nearly as important as physical conditioning. Having access to detailed guidebooks, maps, other hikers' trail journals, on-line forums and chatrooms—in short, a plethora of information beforehand, all easily accessible via the Internet—lends an air of predictability, of reduced uncertainty regarding an endeavor like hiking the Colorado Trail. I've found that for most things in life, the Information Age which provides us so much data and answers at such lightening speed also has created an expectations gap whereby we think computers can do more than they're currently capable of.

And then there's the simple axiom that one must take the time to absorb and internalize all of the available information. For example, I knew I was hiking at high elevations, i.e. over 10,000' in the West and therefore assumed that the Colorado Trail was very similar to California's JMT. Reality: the trails were much more dissimilar than I expected. Had I read the guidebook cover-to-cover as well as other easily accessible sources, I would have realized this. But thankfully unlike Bryson, I wasn't a prisoner of my expectations such that the hike was torpedoed the moment something went wrong or not "according to plan."

Celebration time!

Well before enjoying that brew in the Durango pub, I had reached several conclusions about hiking the Colorado Trail:

The Colorado Trail is very challenging. Not that I expected an "easy" hike, but the Colorado Trail proved formidable. Challenges included the near-constant ups and downs, more-than-occasional rocky footing, dry stretches devoid of good water, stormy weather nearly every day, and, of course, the need to acclimatize. Yet my initial hypothesis proved true: once acclimated, even the Colorado Trail's most difficult stretches were not as arduous as the AT in New Hampshire and Maine. This assertion is more a testimony to the latter's ruggedness than any perceived mellowness of the former.

Hiking the Colorado Trail is very rewarding. What I thoroughly enjoyed about the Colorado Trail was its diversity. I expected and indulged in the rewards of high-elevation alpine meadows with the attendant wildflowers, sparkling clear streams, occasional glistening lakes, critters like ptarmigan, pika and marmots, snowfields, views of distant and near peaks. In addition to these gorgeous features, I took delight in everything else the trail offered, such as: (1) groves of aspens resplendent when bathed by early-morning sun; (2) colorful rock, particularly along the Silverton-to-Durango segment, again accentuated by early morning or late afternoon light; (3) dense forests of evergreens, some too thick to squeeze between; (4) a wide range of plant species including cactus and other succulents; (5) even the seemingly-monotonous dry stretches, in that they made one more appreciative when a long-awaited creek was finally reached; and (6) last-but-not-least, the perpetual celestial motion creating the various shades of gray in the skies, accompanied by near-daily afternoon rains (always threatened, sometimes actually occurring).

In this regard, the Colorado Trail differs quite markedly from the JMT. While spectacular with its own alpine splendor, the JMT is basically a more homogenous trail. You're either in the alpine tundra or slightly below treeline where you cross a stream or river headwaters before hiking up to the tundra again. Hiking the JMT means one does not have to be (usually!) concerned about rain or thunderstorms, but the offset is how the dryness affects your body. Unlike the JMT, where my nostrils and eyes dried out and my skin chafed for the first time of my hiking career, the Colorado Trail never felt excessively dry. Ironically, though, it was the Colorado Trail where water was scarcer in places, a contrast to the water-plentiful but drier atmosphere of the JMT.

Variability is the watchword. Following on from the prior discussion, the Colorado Trail's physical, biological, and geographical diversity, its heterogeneity, is but one manifestation of variability that I experienced on this hike. There's also the weather. Yes, every morning (almost) commenced with bright sunshine. And gray skies inevitably followed, but each day's pattern was never identical. By "pattern," I'm not just referring to the infinite combination of gray hues and cloud shapes but also the timing. Would we never see the sun until the next morning, would it emerge for a hour around 4:30 pm and again for two hours at 7:00? When would the rains start? Would we even get any rain? If so, how much? Intense like a shower or drizzly and misty? Would it just be one period of rain or several? Could there be hail? How about thunder and/or lightening? Might we see rain clouds in the distance but never get wet ourselves? If a hiker desires to be as mentally prepared as possible (I've admitted to such), one must readily accept that the answer is to all these posed scenarios is "any of the above."

Variability also depicts how I felt physically, not just from one day to another but even during the course of a single day. At some point(s) in the hike, I felt fresh, sore, alert, fatigued, strong, sluggish and gasping (before acclimation), wet, dry, hot, cold, sweaty, frost-bitten, hungry, thirsty, sated—often several of these on the same day. And my experience showed that sometimes, the setting (time and place) of these sensations was unpredictable. For example, I normally felt strong in the morning, less so in the afternoon, but hiking Segment 24 found me reversing the "norm" as I strode ahead of Northern Harrier with a briskness that surprised everyone. I felt sated and content after a delicious town meal but at the same time, a sluggishness resulted from excessive indulgence of rich cuisine. How you feel physically can be transformed instantly when, for instance, you suddenly twist a knee or ankle while striding or when you soak your hot, achy feet in a delightful mountain stream. Without doubt, such variation occurs in everyday "off-trail" life as well, but it seems to me that conditions on a backpacking trip in the mountains exacerbate the differences. Certainly, a hiker's options for dealing with abrupt changes in physical circumstances are more limited in a wilderness setting.

And then there's the mental and emotional aspect. Like the changing terrain (up, down, up, down, occasional-but-brief level, up, down), emotions range high and low. It always feels satisfying (and a relief!) to reach a mountain top (even those bereft of views) where a "high" is experienced in more ways than one. Many descriptors are apt: feeling jubilant and on top of the world (not just a mountain), self-satisfaction at your physical ability to ascend several thousand feet, and confidence that you'll conquer what lies ahead. There's joy from partaking of views and scenes that are only attainable by sustaining the sweat and strain of the ascent. There's even a bit of elitistism in knowing that you've done something that (sadly) few Americans are capable of.

Other "highs" followed a drink of fresh water from a mountain stream, hiking through and admiring the splashes of color from the alpine *flora*, observing animals in all of the trail's ecosystems, finishing a segment or attaining a milepoint (100 miles, 200 miles, etc.), feeling the sweat dry from cooling breezes, and interacting with the Trail Angels who helped us in so many way. The completion of a day's hike, preparing and enjoying dinner, viewing the alpenglow of dusk, crawling into a warm sleeping bag, and simply breathing the fresh alpine air—these all led to feelings of satisfaction, joy, contentment, a sense that "I'm where I want to be!" and an awed, humbling reverence for the sacred and divine. Such "highs" more than compensated for the misery of being soaked from a cold rainstorm or encountering an unexpected PUD or grimacing through sore feet or feeling down on yourself for not being as well-conditioned as you'd like.

One sentiment that kept me going during those times when my morale was weakened was the sense of appreciation that the Colorado Trail existed and gratitude for those who worked to make it possible for people like me to hike it. And ultimately for me, the highs won out over the lows. If they hadn't, I likely would not have completed the hike.

Mountain bikers are solid citizens. As my account has shown, all of our encounters with these fellow mountain enthusiasts were positive. Perhaps the anecdote best capsulizing the bikers' ethics occurred as we were crossing a secondary road shortly before entering one of the Colorado Trail's six Wilderness Areas. A forward-facing cyclist sat on his bike intensely studying a map. As we drew close, he turned around and began wheeling back toward us.

"How you doin'? Forget something?"

"No, just figuring out the road route to ride around the Wilderness."

His tone was matter-of-fact, harboring no resentment, no sense of an entitled "right" to bike through Wilderness Areas, through which bicycles are prohibited. In short, he was following the rules without complaint. No hint surfaced that his experience in the Great Outdoors was somehow compromised or rendered less-than-satisfying by following these rules. Perhaps he was also a hiker, or at least appreciated those who partake of the wilderness on their two feet. Perhaps he recognized that trails, especially those in Wilderness Areas, don't just magically happen; it takes hard work by people, traveling to remote locations without benefit of modern power tools.

No hierarchy exists regarding hikers *vis-a-vis* mountain bikers. The practitioners of each recognize and affirm the strenuous physical demands of the other. My hunch is that this mutual respect stems from the sense that our commonalities are stronger than our differences. We both enjoy the mountain outdoors via nonmotorized means, entailing physical exertion. We appreciate the role, indeed the very concept and existence, of public lands set aside for conservation and aesthetics. We know that notwithstanding the fine efforts of private organizations, an example being land trusts like the Nature Conservancy, it is only through governmental action that large swaths of recreational lands are preserved such that future generations may also experience the joys of Creation, and that Nature's nonhuman denizens may also flourish.

Occasionally, I'll read negative stories about mountain bikers in some on-line forum or magazine. I don't define a problem based on mere anecdotes of irresponsible behavior. Do mountain bikes hasten the erosion of trails? For some of the steep sections carved into gravel, I suppose the answer is affirmative. At a point, heavy trail usage by any means—hikers, bikers, horse riders, motorized vehicles—has an impact. However, mountain bikers and their organizations contribute to trail construction and maintenance. They're active in the Colorado Trail Foundation.

The foundation's guidebook addresses mountain biking in a positive manner, allowing that the sport is one of several ways to partake of the Colorado Trail. Per the book:

"Most mountain bicyclists are responsible trail users and their thoughtfulness is appreciated. Also appreciated are the efforts by cyclists to be courteous to other trail users and to slow down when encountering hikers and riders and to pass responsively...Cyclists who avoid skidding are also appreciated..."

So was our experience with bikers an aberration? No, I don't think so. In none of our interactions with mountain bikers was the letter or spirit of the guidebook's concept violated.

Colorado Trail communities are cool. Leadville, Salida, Silverton, Durango, even tony Breckenridge—what neat places to spend a summer! They're surrounded by mountains and enveloped by clean fresh air. They're architecturally interesting with thriving downtowns where you can walk to locally-owned businesses and dine in restaurants other than the bland, mediocre, Anywhere, USA chains. An atmosphere is pervasive, one which says "We're in the outdoors—that's our thing." All the services a hiker

191

or anyone else would reasonably want are available. That is, unless your "thing" is a large suburban-style indoor shopping mall.

The Colorado Trail is not a "social trail." And that's fine by me.

For those who so seek, most of the AT affords a "wilderness," interact-with-nature experience. However, many AT hikers revel as much in the companionship and fellowship engendered from meeting and making new friends at campsites, shelters, and the hostels of trail towns. From reading AT hikers' journals at the website trailjournals.com, I'm struck by how many of these accounts devote most of their words to the hike's social aspects.

In contrast, the Colorado Trail is not about interacting with people; it's about interacting with nature. Sure, you meet people on the trail; it's not a place for hermits. Of our 36 days spent hiking the 482 miles to Durango, only one day (our fourth) lapsed without encountering another human being. As the trail continued winding its way southwesterly, putting Denver and the "Front Range" urban areas behind us, I thought surely we'd experience more solitude in the Dry Heartland or the stretches on both sides of San Luis Pass, our gateway to Creede. Wrong again! Be they fellow backpackers, day-hikers, mountain bikers, a few horse riders, or even one hunter, other outdoors lovers shared the trail with us.

But we never had the feeling of being crowded among a parade of trail users, aside from ascending over Georgia Pass on a Saturday during a mountain biking sponsored event. Even on that Saturday night, the expected plethora of people at our campsite didn't materialize. In fact, for our nights on the trail, we rarely shared a campsite with others except for Mickey with whom we hiked at the same daily pace over a ten day period.

During our hostel stays, we enjoyed talking with those we met, even if our status as backpackers thru-hiking the Colorado Trail placed us in a minority. Hence the conversations didn't take the form of finding out how far Jim Hiker had come now or whether Lisa Hiker had passed through three days ago or news that Bruce

Hiker abandoned his hike. Perhaps it simply comes down to numbers; there are much fewer people backpacking the Colorado Trail, hence less opportunities for social interaction. Aside from Bill Appel's roadside setup of snacks and drinks, the Colorado Trail doesn't feature organized "hiker feeds" or trail festivals or kickoff events or a core of "lifers" whose lives revolve around trail presence every year, at least not visibly to us hikers.

I don't mind meeting fellow trail enthusiasts and I enjoy talking with those I encounter while hiking or staying in the hostels. But social interaction is not the reason that I hike, whether it's this hike of the Colorado Trail or any other.

* * * * *

MY WONDERFUL PHOTOS buttress the many fond memories of the Colorado Trail experience. But as Northern Harrier and I joked, why is it that we don't take pictures of struggling uphill on steep slopes? Or what about the blisters? How about those rockfields, especially the talus slopes? And rain? No pictures of the heavy rainstorms that first day out of Silverton on what was supposed to be a "drier" stretch. And then there was the angst of seeking water in certain dry segments.

Leaving the Dry Heartland for the high peaks.

The point is that as weeks, months, and eventually years roll by, the glasses become more rose-colored—if you let them. Hik-

193

ing the Colorado Trail was fun, exciting, gorgeous, picturesque—the superlatives roll out.   It was also sweat, stress, and
soreness but ultimately rewarding—both for savoring the beautiful
works of nature that we saw, heard, and smelled along the way, and
the sense of accomplishment. We had sought to hike 482 miles in
the Colorado Rockies, and we had succeeded.

Final Thoughts

"...Consider the lilies of the field, how they grow; they neither toil nor spin, yet I tell you even Solomon in all his glory was not clothed like one of these."

Matthew 6:28 (New RSV)

"Lord, how Thy wonders are displayed, where'er I turn my eye,
If I survey the ground I tread, or gaze upon the sky...
There's not a plant or flower below, but makes Thy glories known..."

Issac Watts
1674—1748

"Nature is a revelation of God; Art a revelation of man."

Henry Wadsworth Longfellow

"Never lose an opportunity of seeing anything that is beautiful; for beauty is God's handwriting - a wayside sacrament. Welcome it in every fair face, in every fair sky, in every fair flower, and thank God for it as a cup of blessing."

Ralph Waldo Emerson

B EFORE I HAD ABSORBED any of the above quotations, my unartistic, unscientific eye often marveled at how the natural world evoked a beauty that no human could replicate. For example, when I've snorkeled over the coral reefs in Australia, Hawaii, and the Carribean, I've observed scores of colorful tropical fish. Whether I've seen them in their natural habitat or in aquariums, I've never regarded them as anything but spectacular. Yet could the best artist arrange the same colors in a manner that wouldn't look gaudy or tasteless? My faith in God does not incorporate Christian fundamentalism (else how could I quote Longfellow and Emerson?) but one does not have to believe in a "Young Earth," six-day Creation story nor subscribe to an inerrant Bible to see the Divine hand behind the glories of nature.

And so it was with the Colorado Trail, beginning, of course, with the wildflowers. No matter what color scheme appeared on the landscape, the sense of design was perfect. Every combination of color hues was artistic; there was no clashing of the "wrong" combinations of pinks, yellows, reds, blues, purples, magentas, whites, maroons, oranges, burgundies, *et. al.*

Fairy Trumpets complement Trailing Daisies

It was probably near-identical scenes that prompted John Muir to utter "God never made an ugly landscape."

196

I suspect that Muir harbored a broad concept of what constituted "landscape." Not confined to the subject of a still watercolor, "landscape" encompassed all of the land, sea, sky, and their denizens. When I expressed this sentiment to a new friend—another lover of the outdoors whom I met through hiking circles—she recalled a similar feeling when looking at the ocean. Different shades of blue made up the sky and sea, the differences becoming more apparent at the horizon where they touched. Pondering this scene for a moment, she said "You know, I wouldn't wear a skirt of one blue and a sweater of the other—they wouldn't go together at all. But here standing on the beach, looking at the sky and ocean, they were perfect together." She gets it.

Granted while hiking, the bias is to bright sunshine and cobalt-clear skies. But how could one fail to appreciate the sublime beauty as the transition began, usually in late morning, to the myriad and ever-changing shades of gray? Why, after all, is black-and-white photography so highly acclaimed as an artistic endeavor? What best captures the "landscape" of the heavens, the exquisite design of the Creator?

In his book *The Heart of Christianity*, theologian Marcus Borg writes of "thin places," a concept originating in early Celtic Christianity. People are human, God is divine; there's a separation. Such separation can be characterized as a wall or curtain or veil. Thin places are where this barrier is "thinned" or even lifted to bring us into contact with God. Not everyone's thin place is the same. For some, it's physical houses of worship. For others, it's in the mountains or the seashore or the desert or a simple walk in the country or forests. Thin places are not necessarily physical locations; they can include music or poetry or interactions with people or rituals. And for many people, it's some or all of the above. These examples of thin places are not necessarily mutually exclusive.

I've already stated that hiking the Colorado Trail was physically and mentally challenging, but the rewards were many. One such reward was experiencing the trail and all that it offered, especially the spectral range below and the shades of gray above, as a "thin place" whereby I sensed the Divine presence.

* * * * *

"Here is your country. Cherish these natural wonders, cherish the natural resources, cherish the history and romance as a sacred heritage, for your children and your children's children. Do not let selfish men or greedy interests skin your country of its beauty, its riches or its romance." — Theodore Roosevelt

I HAVE SUNG THE PRAISES of the Colorado Trail Foundation throughout this book. It's patently obvious that the Colorado Trail owes its existence to the women and men who, working through the foundation and its predecessors, dedicated their lives to planning, building, and maintaining the trail. Indeed, the foundation has been a force that gave us, the public, this magnificent trail.

However, credit must also be granted to another force, for in order to construct a trail, the land must be available in the first place. So we who hike trails or pursue other forms of outdoor recreation on public lands must salute Theodore Roosevelt, Gifford Pinchot, John Muir, and other giants of the conservation movement. These heroes did more than simply harbor a vision. They also took action by setting aside lands which became national parks, national forests, national wildlife refuges, and national monuments. The 230 million acres of public lands protected during Roosevelt's administration bestowed a legacy that all of us enjoy to this day. The eight national forests through which the Colorado Trail passes trace their philosophical lineage to Roosevelt's achievements in conservation, as well as his hearty embrace of nature and the outdoor life.

Although the concept and actuality of public lands was established more than a century ago, many national forests, monuments, wildlife refuges, recreation areas, and even parks have always been threatened by special interests, right up to this day. The conservation ethic that Theodore Roosevelt championed was not wholly accepted in its time and still isn't now in certain quarters. Elected officials in state legislatures and the U.S. Congress, as well as recent Presidential candidates, have supported measures to dispose of "excess" federal lands, including, incredibly, national parks. And in all cases, the politicians who push this legislative agenda and the think tanks who provide the intellectual rationale are funded by the same extractive industry groups that Roosevelt and Pinchot battled over 100 years ago.

My concern is that based on conversations I've had with fellow hikers, many take for granted the continued availability of the trail upon which they trod, and don't even realize the threats or think about where their elected representatives or candidates stand on matters involving public lands. In our hikes, we may revel in the natural environment, praising it for the beauty and solace that the forest, mountains, desert, etc. give us. However, we should also be mindful of another, wider environment: that which encompasses culture, history, law, public policy debates, current events, and values. We can't blithely hike in a vacuum without connecting the dots between the trail under our feet and the bigger picture "environment" that envelopes our nation and society.

* * * * *

BARELY A WEEK AFTER stepping off the trailhead near Durango, I was backpacking again. This time it was the 230-mile Superior Trail in Minnesota, a beautiful and scenic trail in its own right, even though the only common element with the Colorado Trail was the presence of mosquitoes. Burgeoning blisters, including a pair on the backs of my heels, threatened infection in addition to infusing pain, resulting in curtailment of the hike only 20 miles short of completion.

In the weeks that followed, the wonders of the Information Age enabled me to connect with Mickey, Tyler, Mike, and Austin, all of whom successfully completed their Colorado Trail hikes. As fellow "hiking lifers," all of them will find themselves on a trail again, sooner rather than later as their schedules permit.

Weeks turned into months, eventually leading to additional backpacking trips including 46 miles on the Ozark Highlands Trail in Arkansas, 70 miles on the John Muir Trail in California, 70 miles on the Northville-Placid Trail of New York's Adirondack region, and 85 miles on the Allegheny Trail in West Virginia, with Northern Harrier accompanying me on the latter. Entering my Medicare years, I still have plans to trek with my food and shelter needs hoisted on my back while I'm able. So many trails, so little time...

Will my future treks ever entail hiking a trail comparable to the Colorado Trail's length? 482 mountainous, challenging miles? After this hike's successful completion, I felt ready to take on something even longer—maybe 600-700 miles of the PCT. Not right away, of course. I craved some rest. But a weary body was secondary to buoyed confidence and spirits. Both sentiments temper over time. Blisters, joints, and overall body stress dissipate while feelings and inclinations level off. If I backpack the PCT, it will be as a section-hiker with no chunk longer than 700 miles. I suspect that with respect to length, the Colorado Trail will remain my personal #1. But then again, in all honesty, I must admit that I really don't know.

What I do know is that I will never forget those 38 days in the Rocky Mountains, whether I hike another 10,000 miles or whether something occurs tomorrow that curtails my hiking for all time. It was, and still is, a time to savor and celebrate a most wonderful, rewarding experience on all fronts—physical, mental, emotional, and spiritual. And I cherish it virtually every day.

Acknowledgments

NEITHER THE HIKE nor the book would have been possible without valuable contributions from many people, whether deliberately by design or unwittingly by happenstance. I owe a tremendous round of thanks to the following:

To every person involved with the Colorado Trail Foundation, from the early visionaries and trail builders like Gudy Gaskill to present day volunteers who give of their time for trail maintenance, planning, coordinating with the U. S. Forest Service, reaching out to the communities both close to home and beyond Colorado and countless other tasks. A special thanks to Bill Manning, the foundation's Executive Director for juggling all the responsibilities of running a volunteer organization with little staff support while still finding time to hike the trail. It's one thing to read about the trail and hear from trail users but nothing beats the firsthand experience of finding out for yourself! Meeting Bill while hiking the trail was one of my highlights.

To the many Trail Angels who helped us along the way, nearly all of whom simply appeared at the right place and right time to offer a ride or a drink or shelter. It started on our third day with the young homeless guy who drove us back to the trail from Buffalo Creek and Zero-Zero's friend Dee who phoned Northern Harrier's wife Charlene to assure her of our safety. There was the guy who gave us the ride from/to Kenosha Pass and Jefferson for our second resupply stop and the family who invited us to wait out a hailstorm under their canopy. We were thankful for Bart and his family who drove us back to the trail from Twin Lakes and for the several folks who gave us water including mountain bikers and day-hikers. We won't forget Bluebird who drove us to the Salida hostel nor the family from Texas who gave us a ride all the way to Creede along the bumpy, high-clearance Forest Service road. We greatly appreciated the drivers who picked us up on our unexpected hitch from Spring Creek Pass to Creede as well as the firefighter who drove us to Silverton. It was a pleasure to meet Ernie Norris on our last day and our good fortune at his being there at the southern terminus and driving us to Durango. And of course Bill Appel for his goodies and shelter in the middle of the Colorado Trail's most desolate stretch.

To our two special Trail Angels: Northern Harrier's lifelong friend Tom Downing who drove all the way from Denver to pick us up in Durango and my long-time friend Keith Davis for accommodating us in his Evergreen home the night before, storing my car safely, driving us to the start of the trail, and putting me up at hike's end.

To Paul "Mags" Magnanti for his comprehensive and always-current on-line guide to the Colorado Trail and his helpful contributions on the website Whiteblaze.net. Mags also has encouraged me in this book endeavor with helpful thoughts and his always-positive demeanor.

To all those who reviewed drafts of this book and provided invaluable and constructive comments which, without question, have made this a better book. I appreciate the insight from Dennis "K1YPP" Blanchard who conveyed his knowledge and experience in writing and publishing a book of this genre. In addition, he reviewed an early draft and offered helpful suggestions. Peter Nunes, who thru-hiked the Colorado Trail the year after me, also reviewed and commented on an early draft. Rick "Handlebar" Ostheimer, an experienced "Triple Crown" backpacker, read the entire text cover-to-cover and provided both editorial and substantive input. I received excellent suggestions on phraseology and style for the first half of the book from Anna "Mud Butt" Huthmaker, and from Deb "Maw-ee" Tucker on the entire book. My niece, Martha Cooke White, a professional journalist, provided both important editorial assistance and highly useful advice from the perspective of a non-hiker. The thorough review by Heather Thompson Wade has saved me from embarrassment as I learned (or re-learned) that no matter how many times one reviews his own work, a different set of eyes will find mistakes. Diane Napolitano reviewed a later draft and provided valuable insight and perspective, resulting in an improved literary product. Others who read the entire text and provided helpful comments included Judy "Gray Jay" Young, Mickey Williamson, the Rev. Kristy Ehlert, Deb de-Peyster, and Mags. A simple yet critical suggestion regarding the book's subtitle was offered by Andrea DePalatis. Thanks to all of you! Any remaining errors are solely mine.

To Ann Bowe whose abiding and steadfast friendship helped me immeasurably in dealing with a personal crisis as this book was nearing completion.

And finally, a Rocky Mountains-sized thanks to Northern Harrier for putting up with me for 482 miles plus 2,500 miles of driving to Colorado and back. In response to a few people's questions "Are you guys still friends," I could unequivocally answer "Yes!" after 44 years of friendship tested by a difficult and strenuous, but ultimately rewarding hike.

Appendices

Appendix 1 — Daily Mileage on the Hike

Date	Destination	Miles
Sunday, July 24	Indian Creek Trailhead (Start of Hike)	
Sunday, July 24	Bear Creek	5.2
Monday, July 25	Campsite near Chair Rocks	12.1
Tuesday, July 26	Tramway Creek	12.6
Wednesday, July 27	Lost Creek Meadow	15.8
Thursday, July 28	Rock Creek	15.2
Friday, July 29	Jefferson Creek	13.8
Saturday, July 30	Swan River North Fork	13.7
Sunday, July 31	CO Rt. 9 Breckenridge	13.2
Monday, August 1	Copper Mountain	14.5
Tuesday, August 2	Jacque Creek	3.5

Date	Destination	Miles
Wednesday, August 3	Campsite, Mile 20.8, Segment 8	15.6
Thursday, August 4	Tennessee Pass, U.S. Rt. 24	4.6
Friday, August 5	Glacier Creek	14.1
Saturday, August 6	Herrington Creek	16.4
Sunday, August 7	Stream, Mile 16.7, Segment 11	13.4
Monday, August 8	Pine Creek	11.2
Tuesday, August 9	Silver Creek Lakes	14.3
Wednesday, August 10	Dry Creek	13.7
Thursday, August 11	Sand Creek	16.9
Friday, August 12	U.S. Rt. 50	10.4
Saturday, August 13	Zero Day in Salida	0
Sunday, August 14	Marshall Pass Trailhead	14.1
Monday, August 15	Dry camp, Mile 3.7, Segment 17	19.1

Date	Destination	Miles
Tuesday, August 16	Campsite beyond Pine Creek	18.5
Wednesday, August 17	Cochetopa Creek, Segment 19	19
Thursday, August 18	Cochetopa Creek, Segment 20	14.3
Friday, August 19	San Luis Pass (Creede)	5.1
Saturday, August 20	Spring Creek Pass, CO Rt. 149	14.8
Sunday, August 21	Segment 22 yurt	8.7
Monday, August 22	Segment 23 lake	14.2
Tuesday, August 23	Elk Creek miner's cabin	17.6
Wednesday, August 24	Molas Pass, U.S. Rt. 550	12.8
Thursday, August 25	Zero Day in Silverton	0
Friday, August 26	Cascade Creek	15

Date	Destination	Miles
Saturday, August 27	Dry camp, Mile 10, Segment 26	15.9
Sunday, August 28	Campsite at Segment 27 view	13.2
Monday, August 29	Junction Creek campsite	15.4
Tuesday, August 30	Durango Trailhead	14.4
	Total Mileage	482

Appendix 2 — The Colorado Trail's 28 Segments

Seg. No.	Ending Point (North-to-South Direction)	Miles
	Waterton Canyon (Northern Terminus)	
1	South Platte Canyon	16.8
2	Little Scraggy Trailhead (FS Road 550)	11.5
3	Wellington Lake Road (FS Road 560)	12.2
4	Long Gulch	16.6
5	Kenosha Pass (US Rt. 285)	15.1
6	Gold Hill Trailhead (CO Rt. 9, access to Breckenridge)	32.9
7	Copper Mountain (CO Rt. 91)	12.8
8	Tennessee Pass (US Rt. 24, access to Leadville)	25.4
9	Timberline Trailhead	13.6
10	Mt. Massive Trailhead (FS Road 110)	13.6
11	Clear Creek Road	21.5
12	North Cottonwood Creek	18.5
13	Chalk Creek Trailhead	22.8
14	US Rt. 50 (access to Salida)	20.4
15	Marshall Pass (FS Road 200)	14.3
16	Sargents Mesa (FS Road 855)	15.2

Seg. No.	Ending Point (North-to-South Direction)	Miles
17	CO Rt. 114	20.4
18	Saguache Park Road	13.8
19	Eddiesville Trailhead	13.7
20	San Luis Pass (access to Creede)	12.7
21	Spring Creek Pass (CO Rt. 149, access to Lake City)	14.8
22	Carson Saddle	17.2
23	Stony Pass (FS Road 737)	15.9
24	Molas Pass (US Rt. 550, access to Silverton)	20.2
25	Bolam Pass Road (FS Road 578)	20.9
26	Hotel Draw Road (FS Road 550)	10.9
27	Kennebec Trailhead (FS Road 571)	20.6
28	Junction Creek Trailhead (access to Durango)	21.5

Appendix 3 — Glossary and Acronyms

Alpenglow - The effect of end-of-the-day light from the waning sun shining back on mountains opposite from where the sun is setting, usually ranging from crimson to faint pink or orange.

AT - Appalachian Trail, a footpath following the Appalachian chain between Springer Mountain, Georgia and Mt. Katahdin, Maine totaling 2,184 miles. The AT was designated a National Scenic Trail under the National Trails System Act of 1968, as amended.

CDT - Continental Divide Trail, a National Scenic Trail along the Rocky Mountains following the Continental Divide between the Mexican and Canadian borders.

Colorado Trail Foundation - The non-profit organization that manages the Colorado Trail, engaging in such activities as maintenance, route planning, community outreach, publications, and coordination with the U.S. Forest Service.

Forest Service - Shorthand for the U.S. Forest Service. A component of the U.S. Department of Agriculture, the Forest Service manages the 193 million acres of the nation's National Forests.

Fourteener or 14er - A Colorado mountain whose elevation exceeds 14,000'. Climbing the 14ers is a popular recreational activity in the state.

National Scenic Trail - A trail designated in accordance with the National Trails System Act of 1968. NSTs are 100 miles or longer, continuous, primarily non-motorized routes of outstanding recreation opportunity. Such trails are established by Act of Congress.

Nero Day - A day in which very few miles are hiked and very little time is taken. Normally, a nero day falls either on the day the hiker arrives at a stop or the departure day from either a town or the start of the hike. The term is an amalgamation of a **ne**arly ze**ro** day (refer to Zero Day definition below).

PCT - Pacific Crest Trail, a National Scenic Trail along the Sierra and Cascade Ranges in California, Oregon, and Washington between the Mexican and Canadian borders.

PEE - Principle of Erroneous Expectations, a term coined by the author which states that an ascent that you didn't expect or were surprised by is more difficult physically than an ascent that you anticipated, even if they're of equal length and steepness.

PUD - Pointless Up and Down, an intervening ascent and descent of little scenic value itself which "gets in the way" of hiking to one's goal. Often, a long ascent or descent will feature PUDs in the middle, making the total gross elevation change greater.

Saddle - A relatively low point on a ridgetop between two higher peaks, not at a great distance from each other.

Slackpack - During the course of a long, multi-day hike, a slackpack is a day-hike for part of the trail which thus does not entail camping for the night, and which is easier because the hiker need only carry a day pack as opposed to a full backpack. It requires some sort of transportation arrangements for at least one end of the hike. Depending on a trail's access points, some trails may be slackpacked in their entirety or most of their length.

Switchback - Stretch of trail routed at an angle ("sideways") on steep slopes to minimize erosion and render the slope more gradual.

Talus Slope - A steep incline covered with large, jagged rocks with virtually no earth showing and devoid of vegetation.

Thru-hike - A hike of a trail in its entirety in one trek. Except in jest, the term isn't used for short trails which can be hiked in one day.

Trail Angel - A person who helps other hikers, usually unexpected, unplanned, serendipitous, and sometimes unwitting. Trail Angels may range from fellow hikers to persons from the "general public" who have never hiked a mile.

Trail Magic - When unexpected acts of kindness are bestowed upon hikers, usually provided by Trail Angels but sometimes arising from fortuitous developments.

Triple Crown - The three major long-distance, north-south National Scenic Trails in the U.S., consisting of the Appalachian Trail, Continental Divide Trail, and Pacific Crest Trail. One who has hiked all three is termed a "Triple-crowner."

Wilderness Area - Tract of federally-owned land—usually part of a National Park or National Forest—set aside by Act of Congress pursuant to the Wilderness Act of 1964. In Wilderness Areas, human activities are severely restricted, in keeping with the Act's mandate to manage such areas "...where the earth and its community of life are untrammeled by man, where man himself is a visitor who does not remain."

Yogi - A verb which falls between begging and hinting, it contains elements of both. Refers to a hiker attempting to persuade non-hikers to offer something the hiker needs such as a ride or food.

Zero Day - A rest day in the middle of a long-distance, multi-day hike in which no, i.e. zero miles are hiked.

Appendix 4 — References and Links

Colorado Trail Foundation
710 10ᵗʰ St. Suite 210
Golden, CO 80401
(303) 384-3729
www.ColoradoTrail.org

Responsible for overall management of the Colorado Trail including planning, construction, maintenance, coordination with the U. S. Forest Service and other public agencies, and community outreach.

US Forest Service
Rocky Mountain Region
740 Simms Street
Golden, CO 80401
(303) 275-5350
http://www.fs.usda.gov/main/r2

All eight of the National Forests through which the Colorado Trail passes are administered by the Forest Service's Rocky Mountain Region. News updates, maps, and other information may be obtained from this office as well as links to each individual National Forest and Ranger District.

Paul Magnanti's Colorado Trail End-to-End Guide
www.pmags.com/colorado-trail-end-to-end-guide

A comprehensive planning guide to the Colorado Trail with descriptive information on the trail, resupply points, communities along the trail, transportation options, and other facts. Mags' site provides up-to-date first-hand accounts of recent experiences and links to a variety of other sources.

Yogi's Colorado Trail Handbook
Yogi's Guidebooks
www.pcthandbook.com

The first edition of this guide was published after my hike and I have not reviewed it firsthand. Nevertheless, Jackie McDonnell aka "Yogi" is both an accomplished hiker (Triple Crown and more) and author of books dealing with planning long-distance hikes. Everything I have heard points to this guide as being an excellent resource.

Erik the Black's Colorado Trail Pocket Atlas
Blackwoods Press
www.blackwoodspress.com

Erik Asorson aka "Eric the Black" has authored several on-line guides to Western long-distance trails including the Colorado Trail which he has thru-hiked. Like Yogi's guide, Erik's book is recent (post my hike). More than just a series of maps, the Atlas provides elevation profiles and details on services offered in communities along the Colorado Trail corridor.

On-line Websites
www.WhiteBlaze.net
www.TrailJournals.com
www.Postholer.com

The first site, while dedicated to the Appalachian Trail as the name implies, includes information on most long distance hiking trails. A series of forums address non-AT trails including an entire forum dedicated to the Colorado Trail. With over 40,000 members,

218

White Blaze provides a wealth of experience, insight, and perspectives. The other two sites also provide forums for trail discussions as well as hikers' on-line trail journals.

About the Author

S INCE HIS FIRST BACKPACKING trip in 1977, Bill Cooke ("Cookerhiker" to his hiking colleagues) has hiked thousands of miles on trails long and short, east, west and central. He finished hiking the 2,184 mile Appalachian Trail in 2005, an effort that encompassed nearly three decades. At 482 miles, the Colorado Trail thru-hike represents his longest continuous trek. Prior to his retirement in 2003, Bill's career with the federal government spanned 32 years, most of which were spent with the U. S. Environmental Protection Agency where as a CPA, he worked in a number of different positions in the accounting and financial management field. He continues to explore trails afar and near his Lexington, Kentucky residence, including Kentucky's 300-mile Sheltowee Trace where he hikes and performs trail maintenance.